OPENING

Collected Writings of William Segal

1985–1997

Continuum New York

1998

The Continuum Publishing Company
370 Lexington Avenue
New York, NY 10017

Published in association with Green River Press
New York, New York

Copyright © 1998 by William Segal

All rights reserved.
No part of this book may be reproduced,
stored in a retrieval system, or transmitted
in any form or by any means,
electronic, mechanical, photocopying,
recording, or otherwise,
without the written permission of
The Continuum Publishing Company.

ISBN 0-8264-1103-7
Library of Congress Catalog Card Number: 98-71491

Part I	Opening 13
Part II	The Structure of Man 43
Part III	The Middle Ground 71
Part IV	Conversations 89
Part V	The Ten Oxherding Pictures 135

Author's Note

This book was compiled from notes, commentaries, and observations made over a period spanning some twenty years—from the 70's to the 90's. Ideas and "models for a new universe á la Gurdjieff" do not appear in each decade, and since first encountering Gurdjieff's ideas I was struck by their profundity and relevance. Tested in my own experience I was increasingly drawn to acknowledge their essential truth.

What follows is hardly a literary effort as much as a series of observations on the life of a man of our time. These observations may be of help to those who wish to know themselves, to understand better the human structure, its limitations and its possibilities. They aim to prepare one for a more intelligent, more conscious participation in the transformative process—in short, to indicate a way toward fulfilling one's role as a true human being.

— WILLIAM SEGAL

Mind unchanging, observes and changes.
We meet in stilled mind, not in changes.

If we open a book intuitively we
open to the page which is for us.

Preface

WILLIAM SEGAL has chosen his words, one by one. Patiently, he has assembled them, intent on their meaning, their multiple meanings, their fine energy and their subtlety. Now he stands in the marketplace, the voyage complete, coming toward us, his hands outstretched, those hands that have helped trees to flower, generous as always. He opens to us, he shares what he knows, what he perceives, what he has discovered within himself, in his silence; in his unity of body and mind. He goes to the center, to that "Grund" that Meister Eckhart evokes. Scattered before us, all around us, lies treasure. During the long voyage, and during the interval and exercise of stop, he has collected, gathered. Now he gives.

And he is a painter, too. Attentive, loving the simple things, he traces the outlines of a flower, a fruit, a face. Working from that same attentive center and established in that same silence, he finds the harmonies in colors and light. So he brings forth that "invisible reality" with which the world is so mysteriously imbued. And makes it tangible, for our joy.

—GEORGES DUBY (1920–1979)
Translated by Cornelia Schaeffer

I
OPENING

The world is filled with invisible realities.
But, if people do not see or hear,
then these realities do not exist.

"...therefore I am my own first cause, both of my eternal being and of my temporal being. To this end I was born, and by virtue of my birth being eternal, I shall never die. It is of the nature of this eternal birth that I have been eternally, that I am now, and shall be forever. What I am as a temporal creature is to die and come to nothingness, for it came with time, and so with time it will pass away. In my eternal birth, however, everything was begotten. I was my own first cause, as well as the first cause of everything else. If I had willed it, neither I nor the world would have come to be! If I had not been, there would have been no god. There is, however, no need to understand this."

—MEISTER ECKHART

OPENING

Sometimes, I find a place in myself. I know where I stand inside. For a moment I can know that I am here, open to a wider view of existence; watchful, conscious of the one who bears my name. Certainly this is not my habitual place, not the everyday order to which I belong.

Rereading Eckhart's words, it flashes in my mind that one must be bold, even reckless in spiritual matters…or must one be cautious? I may grasp the implications of taking my place as a true human being, of dehypnotizing, of awakening to another view of myself…still, there is a question: What is required of me, what are the first steps to the place where, as Eckhart says, God's is-ness is my is-ness, neither more nor less.

To wake up to
who we are
what we are here for.

To make all life
more poetical, more sane
more living, loving.

To experience
the true of all things
this moment…
this moment…
this moment.

Listening to the silence
each part of body/mind
penetrated, filled
stilled,
each part, sensitive,
opens to the presence.

A marriage of body/mind/still
three blending to one.

Unity/multiplicity
a single presence.

All ways
all methods of training
directed towards
relating to a
changeless, omnipresent energy
keeping attention
turned to
inner stillness.

Reality is
even if we fail to cognize it.
I am,
and I never cease
to be,
no matter how persistently
I fail to remember.

Can I really say
I don't exist?
Who is saying it
if not you?
And who if not you
and I can be?

Change?
difficult to change
difficult to become
what we already are.

Stillness?
all we need
to remember—
the other force
all we need—
to open and
let body and mind
listen.

Attention on still filled structure
listening to the silence
each part of body/mind
is penetrated.

Stilled, sensitive, open
aware of breath
there is a marriage
of body/mind

Opening
we become
unknowing knowers
seers of the worlds
and ourselves
from the viewpoint
of awakened ones.

The mind is able
to discern
the difference
between I am
and I am not.

But mind forgets…
forgets, also, that,
like the body,
it is made to
serve the whole.

Like the body
mind is self-absorbed
has its own agenda.

Does not fulfill
its role
to see
and help
to solve the
human questions
of right living
of right being
of helping humans
to become truly human.

Does not decipher
paradox, riddle of
I am
and I am not.

There is
no division of worlds,
no energies not contained
in the one.

Nobody separate from God,
no body separate from mind
all together is subsumed—
an integrated whole
that cannot be split,
divided or atomized.

There are no saviours
but the fundamental reality
on which we are all
irrevocably based.
The same universal
being-impulse
that gives birth
to material body
opens, unfolds
throughout nature.

This is reason why
we feel kinship
to the earth,
to the trees
and mountains,
to the grass
we tread on.

Opening the Door

We all carry a question: Why am I living? In the substratum of everyone's being we all come to it, have to confront it. Experiencing the swings between moments of happiness and of misery, questions appear.

A man accepts, often with heroic patience and endurance, both necessary and avoidable suffering. When he is against the wall, he seeks the way out. On the other side, surrounded by pleasures, he may ask, "What is reality? Is there something else? Is this all?"

A man meets his life most poignantly in moments of painful contraction and expansion. At those moments he senses the difference between being present and being taken. If he keeps himself open to the question, he will move in what he believes is a fruitful direction.

Many roads will beckon: art, studies, perhaps drugs— other pursuits. He may not find the answer to his fundamental question but he senses that a reality is escaping him; perhaps that something within himself can change existence. Maybe he has a fleeting feeling while listening to a passage of music, or is struck by a word, by nature. Perhaps some flash appears in the midst of love, of sorrow, or joy—a moment of ah...! something is here, strange, wondrous.

And at that moment, a door opens. He may or may not go further. The chances are that the pull of gravity will close the door. He will be shut away from his ever-present possibility. Back to the office and workplace, to vacations, to family, to having good time/bad time, getting and spending. The door may never open again—or will it?

Towards Awakening

People divide themselves by the belief that there is meaning in the universe, or that there is no meaning...that God is or does not exist. If there is an Absolute, it probably knows very well what it is doing, what should be done, and what will be done. What, then, is man's part?

G.I. Gurdjieff's vision of man's destiny is hopeful on one hand, and pessimistic on the other. His contribution was to give back to man hope for meaning in a world in the maintenance and evolution of which he could consciously participate. The coherence of human existence is summed up by the word "harmony," and the concept of divine duty.

Work on oneself, says Gurdjieff, begins with study, observation, and experimentation, and continues as an experience. Just as fire flames what it touches, so consciousness lights up the human being and all things living.

Awareness of oneself, self-remembering, is a step towards awakening a subtle sleeping energy which can infuse form with new life. Freedom is only in formless Self. Not having any form, energy is free to take any form.

There are moments when thoughts, feelings, reactions subside, and, like the calm sea, there is only the vast experience itself. Awareness of an unknowable, undefinable continuum replaces the linear flow of perceptions. Relating to the essence despite the interference of appearances may come suddenly, or may arise gradually, through meditative effort. This is the ascent to which man is invited.

But in order to begin man must be able to view the random dis-pattern of his energies, to give choiceless attention to the moment not time measurable. When man is inwardly still, the silence instructs.

Body and Mind

Each of us feels his existence through his mind and his body. He "is" through these phenomenal aspects of his being. Only on rare, special occasions does he sense—and only dimly—his noumenal side.

Behind his body and mind, through which he is continually affirming and reaffirming himself, his ever-present unchanging reality invisibly sustains him.

Ideally, a man should function from both the phenomenal and noumenal sides of himself, relating and reconciling the multitudinous energy patterns, coming from various levels.

Frustration appears whenever there is a discrepancy between mind and body, when the two are out of step and do not relate harmoniously to each other. Too often a speeded-up tempo carries the mind away ahead of the body—or a constriction in the latter disturbs its relationship to the thinking part.

Seeing this discrepancy is a first step to harmony.

There is an awareness which follows natural flow. Balanced attention, sustained for a brief time, invariably results in the reconciliation of body and mind, sensitizes feelings, and opens the door to another level.

Sensing, the practice of placing one's attention on a specific part or area of the body, expands and deepens the reception of impressions, endows the body's automatized functions with added intelligence.

Sensing oneself, particularly as a whole, paves the way and helps to enlarge the capacity to see the random associations and thoughts which float through the head.

This practice, coupled with observing one's shifting moods and feelings, opens the question of a higher reality behind or within the corporeality one calls "me".

Sensation and Consciousness:

Sensation, consciously or unconsciously experienced, instantly evokes transcursion or passage throughout the whole of the body. To sight, hearing, touch, smell, or taste must be added the muscular (light or heavy), kinesthetic, and sexual senses, the sense of temperature (hot or cold), of time and space, and finally—of consciousness.

Although one has a sense of himself distinct from body/feeling/mind configuration, the activities of the latter obscure and block relationship with one's well-hidden reality. The understanding of this relationship, coming closer to self, is the aim of all work. The preliminary knowledge that one's activities and one's thoughts belong solely to mind/body helps to clear the path.

In stillness one has the sensation of being opened to a more subtle cognition. It is a sensation akin to the one that comes when one is in communication with nature, with great music and art. Sometimes one experiences this energy in the presence of a man or woman with Being, or when an unexpected moment of grace, of sorrow, of shock frees one from routine associations. Suddenly there is an opening to another energy—the unmistakable taste of something higher and truer.

> I can be infinitely more relaxed than I am.
>
> I can be infinitely more sensitive to my sensations.
>
> I can be breathed.
>
> I can be open to a thought from above.

Thoughts

Is there a vibration not ordinarily experienced?
Don't answer. Yes won't do. No won't do.

How not to forget the many possibilities each moment brings? A unique relationship is here, in this present moment. It is a question of calling attention back to yourself, simply being aware of your doing what
you are doing.

Attention is the magnet that draws energy to the right places, and creates harmonious order.

We have been given a mind, we have to know it.
We have been given higher mind, we have to earn it, to find it. We have been given receptivity, we have to develop it.

Sometimes when, through shock, dispersed attention is suddenly collected, one comes to an abrupt awakening, glimpses the relationship between energy and attention. Impressions are received differently, perceptions are wider and sharper. Unexpectedly, another side of oneself is revealed. The value of existence, the existence of all living things, takes on new meaning.

It is the awakening of Self that brings unselfing.

The "is-ness" of each thing contains all and everything.

Attention is an animating principle in each living organism which serves to connect and relate energies with systems of higher and lower orders…a moving entity with possibilities for diminishing or expanding intensity.

Just as there is a network of communication, a worldwide sharing of ideas and applications, a sharing on a psychic level is also taking place among us.

Nobody acts without influencing others. If one rises in his understanding, he becomes a substantial help to others. If he falls, he harms. Outside of intentional cooperation there is always constant, unconscious cause and effect—unwitting influences that can and do embrace wider circles than we realize.

The Japanese have a saying: When a cow eats grass in Osaka it fills the belly of a horse in the neighboring province of Kyushu. A man who rises in spirit in London helps his fellow men in Walla Walla.

We are called to witness the existence of the finite and the presence of the infinite. Both call, both are here. They only lack a witness to their presence. Witnessing/watching is the quintessential human task. Self-remembering takes man to the highest power.

Thoughts

We suffer from lack of wholeness caused not only by fragmentation and imbalance, but, primarily, by lack of contact with Self, with the reality that is in each one—never born, never dying.

Body/mind/feelings—continually betraying our reality.

Self is to be interpreted not relatively but absolutely. The life of the Self, unconditioned, determines one's everyday life. The misfortune of man is due to the fact that the life of Self does not enter into the life of self.

Most of the time, we put our trust only in our sense perceptions. I look at you. I see you. I even touch you. But I still do not see or touch the essential you. There is a reality to this inner you far beyond sense perceptions. In the same way I fail to recognize my essential self—the reality beyond mind cognition. Perhaps it can only be comprehended through opening to an awakened moment which comes to astonish and bless.

This body of flesh, nerves, electrical impulses, the outer crust of one's fundamental self or being, is the visible manifestation of an eternal reality—mine, yours, ours.

It is the intellect and senses that discriminate.

Will may follow intellect, but love has primacy in the sense that what one loves one chooses, the heart persuading the mind.

Love is the great unifying force, the true binding force. The mutual attraction that exists in the universe binds subatomic particles to make atoms, atoms to make molecules, cells to make organs, planets to make solar systems, solar systems to make galaxies.

The sole reality is consciousness, and consciousness only. What we regard as externally existing is nothing other than consciousness in differentiated, ever-renewing forms.

No matter what the form is, it is rooted in what may be described as the fundamental reality, primordial being. No matter how forms or states differ, this fundamental reality does not lose its identity. Even when we feel lost, estranged from it, it is still communing with us.

Listening quietly to ourselves we know that we are, even though we may not know what we are. Perhaps this is the ultimate knowledge.

Consciousness alone translates into freedom, even into immortality. In an otherwise highly determined universe, only consciousness acts to divinize.

Thoughts

Mind quiet, body devoid of tensions, we function freely, open to the higher that is always present.

To live in the presence of God as if there were no god— open to the present presence.

In each life there are passages which have a special poignancy. Lit up with vivacity, they are invariably marked by concentrated attention.

With attention one sees new relationships.

Watchfulness at the moment of receiving an impression; the deeper an impression enters, the greater its power to work.

"Stop" is active/passive resulting in a halt to mechanical activity…the prelude to a new energy.

Question: on the spectrum of receptivity, where am I now? On the spectrum of responsibility, where am I now?

The paradox of our so-called search is that we are trying to find what is, always was, and always will exist. It is not a question of changing anything—of becoming good, better, or best. It is a question of awakening, of becoming conscious of our consciousness, or conscious of our unconsciousness. Either will do.

The sole effect and direction which work on oneself takes is simply to be what one was destined to be from the very beginning.

The human being exists in a limited time/space field and at the same time is surrounded by and eternally related to the timelessness and limitless.

The secular and the sacred—all forms are manifestations of the formless.

The body is born, matures, and dies. The spirit that infuses the body is never born, never dies.

Reality…always with us!

Where Is Self?

I am sitting here. The doorbell rings. I put down the pen which is writing, take off my glasses, and stand up. My wife calls out, "It is Pascal."

From the first gesture of sitting down to the complex network of feelings initiated by the mention of the visitor's name, a series of inner events has taken place resulting in a number of outer actions which I assume I am doing, and which I call "my" life. For my wife and our visitor Pascal it is the same. Even a casual reflection on the actions, feelings, and thoughts that have been automatically evoked arouses questions of the self, provokes renewal of the eternal query "*Who am I?*"

No matter how strong the belief that my form is myself, it is only the thought or feeling or reaction of the particular moment. But where is my invisible reality? Where is the Self that lies underneath?

Everything I do or say, feel or think, comes through the framework of my form—as if all my actions are a reflection of a reflection in a mirror. Nowhere is my reality present.

Buried and sometimes vaguely glimpsed, sensed as if through a net, lies the unfathomable key to the mystery of Self. The old, ever-new question, "Who am I?" continues to haunt man. As long as he takes phenomenal events as Self he remains in their thrall, at the mercy of the drama which is each individual's destiny.

The first opening to freedom is the seeing of oneself. Even a slight echo of this seeing is felt in a change in the relationships which constitute the events within body/mind.

The Ultimate Illusion

A football match between two leading teams is taking place. There are twenty-two players on the field. The officials, the coaches, the alternates on the sidelines, and the stadium packed crowd sense and respond to the excitement. Present to the spectacle before them, it is understandable that few comprehend the marshalling of forces, the chemical and biological adjustments which determine the reactions that are in motion. Each spectator is subject to an irresistible identification with the play, which brings a blindness to the myriad of interdependent processes that are taking place in himself.

At the moment of highest pitch, of the most intense engagement, each one, embroiled or enthralled by the contest, forgets that at another moment he will be turned to another and different set of relationships.

The phenomenal self as an ever-abiding entity is an illusion, soon to be replaced. Where is the person that comes and disappears in response to the changing inner arrangements, which are, in turn, generated by shifting biochemical and biogenetic interactions?

Just as images reflecting seeming realities appear on a television screen, we are reflections of a reality which for the most part escapes us. Other reflections, family, neighbors, tax collectors, take us for realities in the same way that we perceive them as ultimate solidities.

Such is the great illusion that dominates our thinking and our activities, and effectively prevents us from knowing who we are. To say that we are "such stuff as dreams are made on" is as near as we can come to the truth about ourselves. At the same time, the human inability to accept vthis idea does not interfere with our accepting the reality of our numerous mind images.

Neither does the conversion of the mind images into concrete materialities, such as complex machines and astonishing creations, persuade man that he in turn may be the mind image of a higher reality. Still further from man is the cognition that he himself possesses the solidity of millennia and that his invisible rejected reality is capable of unimagined gestures.

Each human is modeled as a system that can observe, can monitor itself. We are unable to evaluate or regulate our interaction with a higher level which may exist in us unless our own model includes this reality. And we cannot know what is real without taking into account ourselves as measuring apparatuses, apparatuses that may vary and change in their ability, capacity, and competence in the distinctions they make.

No cognition or interaction with unknown energies is possible unless it is pre-scribed in the organism. In other words, the only reality (or realities) is our perception of it.

As you read, speak, or listen, you may be able to observe the movement, the flow of your thoughts. You see reaction, agreement, negation—the intrusion of ideas, of moods. At the same time you may be able to be aware of a permanent background, the feeling of an unchanging, ever-present current in yourself.

A thought, a feeling that occupied you a moment ago will disappear, inevitably to be replaced by another. Still you are always in touch with a background—you…"I".

"Stilled, one stops; stopping, one lets go; letting go, one passes through; passing through, one is re-born."

Elaborating New Energy Patterns

How to bring qualitative materialities and energies from other levels into our world? Consider the question from the point of view of the law of attraction, of "like attracting like."

Man as a microcosmos, has in himself all the stuff of the macrocosmos, of the universe itself. What we now possess, however, are merely trace materials, so minute in quantity as to be almost non-existent, and more or less inaccessible to us. Nevertheless it is through what we are that we have the possibility of attracting significant higher elements. At moments of awareness, the connecting link is present. Existing high energies in us are focused and adjusted. We are in equilibrium, in relation to the worlds above, as well as below us.

An inner stop, a pause in the flow of mechanical associations, like an influence from another level, breaks the mechanical flow of associations, freeing and enabling the mind to comprehend more clearly than in its usual busy state. In changed, suspended moments, the mind's energies are free to relate to other currents which are elaborated by the body. No longer do streams of thought particles bar the entry of finer, subtler substances. No longer are potentially harmonious combinations deflected and blocked.

Receptors we are, as well as reflectors, of other worlds.

Further Speculations on Energy and Death

There are parts of man's inner structure that are perfectly adapted to receive forces of a finer nature than those energies which ordinarily fuel man's thoughts, feelings, and perceptions. Most of the time these are covered up by the passage of coarser energies which the organism elaborates in the routine of daily activities. When more sensitive receptors are free to function, there commences an exchange, a blending with more subtle energies which ordinarily pass by and through us, unattended and unused.

Energies which might have been extracted and elaborated at the time of their initial reception, and distilled by their passage through the human frame are rarely utilized. Only in special moments, when feelings arouse states of heightened sensitivity, does effective reception take place.

Death, the stilled state, abruptly ruptures the dynamic energy patterns of the human form. Stoppage, and suspension of the body/brain mechanism may not, however, inhibit the free flow of more subtle energies.

Unknown centers may function freely but briefly after death. The last elaborations of energy leave the body to become part of an enigmatic universal force to which literature and religion give names such as spirit, soul, the absolute. Despite death's disruption, an ultimate energy principle in each human being remains...indestructible, imperishable.

Atoms to galaxies, universe in transformation…

Law of Three, Law of Seven

The teaching of G.I. Gurdjieff places emphasis on two fundamental laws—the law of seven and the law of three—as being the prime factors which determine the flow and transformation of energy and matter. The law of seven is the law of processes; the law of three is the law of relationships.

According to the law of seven, every transformative process in the universe, from the life of a cell to the life of a solar system, unfolds as an octave in seven successive steps. The progression of each octave is determined at two intervals by the presence or absence of appropriate shocks.

According to the law of three, every new arising, every phenomenon, is the result of a combination of three different forces: positive, negative, and neutralizing. Through the study of the manifestations of thought, activity, habits, and desires, it is possible to observe the functioning of this law in ourselves.

From one point of view, and from the perspective of cosmic time scales, the two laws proceed more or less automatically. Involution and evolution, birth, growth, decay, and death take place in fitting sequence. We admire the orderliness of growth and development of things in nature; and yet this order is more or less mechanical. All goes on with minimal conscious participation of the energies and matter that are involved.

For man too there is no self-determined origination. Everything he thinks, does, believes, says, is the result of the blending of impressions and energies received from the outside with the never-ending combinations of ensuing thoughts, acts,

"originations," and previously received and digested impressions and energies. Without the shock of his conscious participation, his growth and development
proceed only up to a point. Although he is a complete cosmos, man is far from being a completed creation.

A simplified example of the law of three: active and passive may be likened to two tennis players facing each other across the net. One is ready to serve, the other to receive. Without the tennis ball there is no game—the ball, the neutralizing force, brings about an interaction of energy.

This principle, well-understood in physics, depicts the basic structure of all interactions: positive and negative electric charges play the parts of the first and second forces; the interaction between them is mediated by the third force—the photon. This and other types of energy exchanges among elementary particles demonstrate that the active and passive forces are interchangeable and transformable one with the other.

The same principle applies to our two natures, the noumenal and the phenomenal, which play the roles of active and passive. They are complementary and interchangeable one with the other. The question is one of right blending, of bringing about an interplay between the two which would result in an opening, a happening (a creation). Seeing is third force. Its first result is letting go of interlocked contractions allowing expansion and opening towards the "new".

The need to experience a different level of being may be seen as initiative, as active force. Inertia, passivity, which characterize our habitual way of being, exists in opposition to this initiative. These two forces will either counterbalance each other, or one will conquer or eventually become too weak for further action. Or they will revolve one around the other producing no result. Conscious attention reconciles the active and passive forces within us.

Can we experience, in a moment, the possibility of bringing these three forces together? In the fusion, activity need not disappear but can result in rhythm as random sounds turn into music. The passive need not disappear, but like silence can promote harmony. Required is an awareness of awareness—consciousness of the buried conscious element in each human being.

All creatures, all substances, may eventually evolve, but the time factor is involved, and man can't wait. For his own and for universal, transformative purposes, he is given a conscience and the possibility of consciousness.

The key is attention. Think only and entirely of what you are doing at this instant and you are free.

"The astonishing thing is not that there exist natural laws, but that the further the analysis proceeds, the fewer the details, the finer the elements to which the phenomena are reduced, the simpler—and not the more complicated, as one would originally expect—the fundamental relations become and the more exactly do they describe the actual occurrences."
—HERMANN WEYL, *The Open World*

Every Moment Beckons

We are continually aligning or relating ourselves to those energies or actions which we perceive as being favorable and desirable. Our bodies take us to food, sex, rest, recreation. Our minds take us towards knowledge of all kinds. Our feelings attract us to the arts, to nature, even to spiritual pursuits. This is all natural and desirable... But is it not strange that we do not, at the same time, turn more frequently to the supreme energy, to the Self veiled within each of us, for the profundity of which we only have human words?

True knowledge, to perpetuate itself, needs living forms. Those who seek it must assimilate it directly by participation of their whole being. It is not the knowledge but the experience of the "other" that a teacher imparts. This becomes yours; when you receive it you can shape it in your own way to meet your particular needs. Our life situations, our make-ups are different. You will use the experience of wholeness to meet your life, not adapt it to my way. This is a living teaching. The way is shown, the experience is passed on like a light from candle to candle. But it is always an individual light.

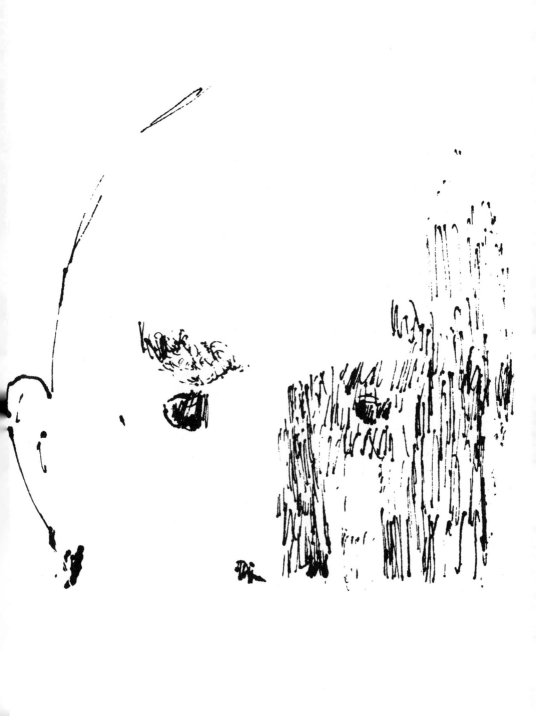

QUIETLY WATCHING, anticipating nothing, I am open to what is here, now. I look at myself reading these words. I read slowly. I see the way I am sitting. I sense my body, the arising and the movement of thoughts, of feelings— the way my breath comes and goes. I am the witness and the witnessing, passively watching and actively being watched.

I see that there can be a further letting go, a beginning relationship to an unchanging inner stillness. Like a white sheet of paper that retains its nature, I remain receptive but unstained, quietly in touch with what is taking place, attention wholly in the moment. Is there help in a stop? In an unfolding to a fresh time/space? Is there a way to be without doing?

Listening to the silence which is present in the stillness I become aware of a new web of relationships, of a unity bringing the body/mind structure to another threshold. I sense that there is another Reality that can be served. Again, a stop.

Will the fragility of my attention survive the experience of turning this page?

II
THE STRUCTURE OF MAN

Each man/woman stands midway between the alpha and the omega of the universe. Shaped and determined by earth forces to which he cannot help but react, he is, at the same time, beckoned by a call coming from higher forces. Between the pull of the earth and the Silence, he is made to comprehend and respond to the cosmos above and to the ones below.

The key with power to change, attention bridges the gap between man and higher forces, sustains and is sustained by the ongoing interplay of body/mind energies. Focusing, sharpening, and heightening receptivity, conscious attention restores and strengthens, makes meaningful, the structure of man.

No Energy Is Isolated

Every creature is an energy system composed of parts or subsystems. Each has its definite place. Each is in movement, constantly changing and inevitably related either upward or downward, no single one existing in isolation. Energy passes down from above in ceaseless movement, like water spilling over a dam, sustaining life in a methodical, foreordained way. There is also an inverse exchange, from lower to higher. With man this depends on the factor of consciousness. All systems have gates to allow for an exchange of energies. For most, however, the gate swings only one way. Man's unique position is that, for him, the gate swings both ways.

All energies are related. No energy exists in isolation, and no energy can remain the same. Even the Absolute manifests in multiform.

Unless an energy system is transformed, it degenerates into a lower form. Rocks dissolve into their constituent minerals. After death flesh decays into its organic compounds. Even the materiality of the sun becomes denser through the fusion of hydrogen to helium. In such an entropic universe, the replacement of coarse for fine, of lead for gold, is inevitable.

However, the disintegration of any energy system can be reversed if the system is related to a level higher than its own. There is a unifying force that integrates and balances all energies. Only through cooperation with and participation in this unifying principle can an energy system be related to higher levels.

This force enables relatively complex systems to respond intelligently to changes that threaten their integrity. A rock has no way of dealing with a flake of acid, but an oyster can create a pearl to neutralize the effects of an intruding grain of sand. On this level, the immortality of an energy system lies in the possible recombinations of its elements. Man has the capacity to cooperate intentionally with this unifying principle. His capacity for conscious attention enables him to fulfill a unique role in the cosmic circulation of energies. Through conscious attention, he participates in the renewal of higher energies, and renews his own. Lower energies are converted to intermediate ones, capable of sustaining the vibrations received from above. The reversal of the entropic tendency of the universe depends on this activity.

The body/mind complex is an energy system which can be related to finer energy patterns or can be disequilibrized to the point of chaos. When one first begins to work with conscious attention one discovers that the subsystems of body, feelings, and mind function inefficiently and disharmoniously. Yet the simple awareness of misalignment may introduce an element capable of binding the disparate parts into an integrated whole. With sustained awareness comes a heightened sensitivity, openness, a quiet mind. Man's structure becomes receptive to the advent of fresh, vivifying energies descending from a mysterious source. This creates a field, where higher energies can transform the lower.

Man may not be cognizant of the possibility of intentionally opening to vibrations from another level. Still, without mankind's conscious participation in a cosmic exchange, the universe is indeed closed. God begins to absent himself from earth. For when man no longer provides the place where higher can meet lower, the latter is cut adrift. The higher, no longer replenished, retreats. All is entropy.

Recognition of man's part in reunifying the fragmented cosmos cannot be reached by thought alone. Only rare moments of complete attention show how, within him, man holds the missing element; how his is the work that sustains creation.

If man is to play his foreordained role — allowing microcosm and macrocosm, phenomena and noumenal, to interpenetrate—he must let go. "The hearing of God's Word," Meister Eckhart has written, "requires complete self-surrender." Paradoxically, the thought that one has something to do in the work of creation is a hindrance to surrender. The highest energy, the fundamental "building block," is already present in each entity. To this energy, every blade of grass owes its innate perfection. Yet, unless the highest in the universe is unveiled through the intermediary energy of conscious attention, the ultimate human purpose will not be fulfilled.

Placed on earth through no determination of his own, can man play his part in the cosmological exchange? For the most part, insensitive to his awesome responsibility, only at rare moments does he occupy his role.

On Transformation

Self-observation and self-remembering are the prime, quintessential processes in the transformation of a human being.

Self-observation is not easy. We are well cushioned from seeing ourselves. Our egoism insulates us; our self-image prevents seeing in depth. I may see a gesture, but do I see where it comes from? I can hear the tone of my voice, but am I able to trace back and observe from where the inflection comes, what thoughts and feelings it is connected with? Do I see the source of a negative emotion? The very question, "What is self-observation?" needs to be kept alive.

Similarly, the idea of self-remembering, of being present at the point of receiving impressions is easy to comprehend; but the experience of being present to more than one or two parts, and of being able to be in touch with an ever-present silence is not for theoretical understanding.

Stillness in the mind, subtlety and sensitivity in the feelings, and a relaxed body need to be in harmonious relationship. With heightened attention, we feel an inner shift, *as if the gaze of the attention regulates and harmonizes different parts*. Simply seeing the imbalance of one part in relation to another is crucial.

Remaining quiet, open, relatively free of negativity, we come to a state which may be called better, even higher. But this state does not last—it just fades away. This loss is caused by the fading of awareness.

Self is always present, but one needs deep stillness to open to it. The physical posture and the body can be of great help. Awakening to the state of mind/body is the first step towards the appearance of "I."

On Thoughts and Thinking

Just as objects, acts, events on the physical plane are the visible results of our invisible thoughts, just as the architect's blueprints or the writer's ideas take shape in the form of buildings or books, so all the myriads of forms in the universe arise from mysterious undifferentiated background. Thinking and thoughts, too, arise from the formless. It is in the nature of the human to be called to thinking—not only by the desires and the senses, but also by his deepest intuition that he is more than a moving, feeling and thinking configuration or apparatus.

Thoughts are forms of matter or energy. They circulate in the atmosphere, stirring up nascent thoughts and feelings already present in us, resulting in new combinations which we call ideas, discoveries, etc… In short, all forms arise from the formless. We are that eternal, changeless, formless at the time that we are the changing, time-bound forms. Questions concerning, "Who am I?" "the sense and aim of living and dying" call us to think—and thinking ultimately leads us to Self.

When thinking is carried out intentionally, when the attention is steadily focused on the subject of thinking, rather than being taken by associations and sporadic impulses, it opens up the subject to its fullness. Steady, unflickering attention can give the thinker the knowledge he wishes to have.

We think because we want something—we want to *know*, to *be* something, to *clarify* something. Generally, thinking is prompted by our desires, senses, and identifications; this "wanting-identification" aspect, which frequently characterizes thinking, means that a certain amount of energy of a high order becomes attached, goes into the thoughts created by the thinking as well as the thinking process.

Gold coins may be raining down from heaven, but if one is not there to receive them, they are of no avail.

Attention Awakens Dormant Energies

The role of a conscious human being is to provide the phenomenal earth world with energies which otherwise would not be effectively transmitted to the creations and units which make up our world. Just as right balance and interaction of energies bring unity, Being appears when harmony and equilibrium replace chaotic imbalance. Being is the universe under God's eye.

Attention is the quintessential medium to reveal man's dormant energies to himself. Whenever one witnesses the state of the body, the interplay of thought and feeling, there is an intimation, however slight, of another current of energy. Through the simple act of attending, one initiates a new alignment of forces.

Maintenance of a conscious attention is not easy. The movement, the obligations of day-to-day existence constantly distract. With no base of operations, no home in one's organism, the attention serves random thoughts, feelings, and appetites which conflict and tyrannize each other.

Sensation of parts or the whole of the body can anchor the attention, provide it with a kind of habitat. The structure, becoming more sensitive, helps to unify attention, so it is less liable to veer into mental channels that consume its power. In turn, perceptions and sensations are quickened, insights are multiplied.

Open to the force of attention evokes a sense of wholeness and equilibrium. One can glimpse a possibility of a state of awareness immeasurably superior to that of the reactive mechanism, an awareness which transcends one's automatic subject/object mode of response.

Freely flowing, the concentrative, transforming effect of conscious attention brings the disparate tempos of the centers to a relatively balanced relationship. Thought, feeling, and sensing are equilibrated under this vibrant, harmonizing influence.

Attention is an independent force which will not be manipulated by one's parts. Cleared of all internal noise, conscious attention is an instrument which vibrates like a crystal at its own frequency. It is free to receive the signals broadcast at each moment from a creative universe in communication with all creates.

However, the attention is not 'mine.' In a moment of its presence, one knows that it does not originate entirely with oneself. Its source surrounded by mystery, attention communicates energies of a quality the mind cannot represent.

One needs to be at the service of conscious attention; one prepares for its advent through active stillness.

In quiet, tension-free moments, man's structure is open to energy flows which are ordinary blocked. In turn, these energies blend with previously received materials, to serve the higher in a wordless, nameless exchange.

Attention is not only mediating; it is transmitting. Giving and receiving, God speaks to man. Receiving and giving, man speaks to God. Just a man's structure needs to be vivified by the infusion of finer vibrations, those very same vibrations require the mixing of coarse material for their maintenance. Without the upward transmission of energies through the intermediary of conscious attention, the universe would give in to entropy.

In man, the smallest deformation of a balanced attention closes down this two-way communications. Alone, the mind cannot maintain it. A relaxed body, too, is needed.

Mid-way between the micro and macrocosmos, man has his part to play. Returning to the body is a gesture of opening to the attention which, beckoned, is ready to serve its cosmological function.

Just as time and eternity continually take each other's measure, man's structure and an unchanging force field interact in a flux relationship, bringing a wedding of earth and changeless heaven.

A Special Time for Our Earth

We are living in a special time. Throughout the world there is a stirring and an interrelation of forces never before experienced by mankind. All around us we see an unprecedented acceleration of the possibilities for change. Power potentials have been released which threaten to upset cosmic balances.

Ironically, the more gigantic and astonishing our manipulation of these energies, the more puerile and insignificant our understanding of them. Philosophers and scientists are coming to agree that not only do we need a deep alteration in the present state of mankind, but that a radical shift depends solely upon our relationship to consciousness— the invisible, fundamental energy behind phenomenal existence.

As one walks the streets of the city, one is struck by the energies manifested through each human being — the results of wishes, emotions, and physical movements, energies in incessant random motion. Inextricably bound to an entire fabric of events, we have no choice but to submit to the rhythm and momentum of our ordinary lives. Yet, in the midst of the flux, a call to consciousness can be heard. Is it possible to accept one's inevitable destiny, and, at the same time, open to the timeless, spaceless, essential movement? Can we microscopic entities, beset by our frailties and mal-training, initiate a radical transformation for ourselves and for the earth?

It is a sensitive task to open to the constantly changing patterns of inner and outer life. Although passivity prevails, possibilities are not limited. We have the help of ideas that can lead to the nurturing of openness. The secret is to use all that is offered, including life's difficulties, to remember the call to consciousness and to develop the will to respond.

There are times when conscience alone, supplementing reason, can bring equilibrium and openness. The realization that one's life is a waste for oneself and for others, that one lives here on earth without fulfilling one's purpose, brings the experience of conscience. Thus touched, one may be moved to another understanding. Change, movement, liberation are possible. But until conscience, deeply buried in the subconscious, is aroused, one may never unveil the feeling needed to create and sustain the human link to another order of energy.

Man as an Energy Field

We seek to awaken to the point where fine energies penetrate, transform, grow, and steer our everyday lives to our hidden reality.

In the sense of an eternal reality which transcends time while entering into it, man's Being is neither subject to, nor needs change. In its absolute meaning, Being (whether yours, mine, the cat's, the mouse's, the tree's, the flower's, a stone's, the earth-clod's) exists outside as well as in time.

Like a magnetic file which attracts iron, each man's structure corresponds to a precise energy field which beckons, repels, and interacts with other energy fields. Despite the experience and the feeling of a permanent 'I' behind his thoughts and movements, these latter, by their ever-changing, dynamic-mechanico nature, tend to blind man to the fact of his Being/Reality.

Unceasingly, at each moment, arcs of energies flow and are exchanged among the different obscuring webs of actions and reactions. Thoughts, feelings, and sensations mesh, intermesh within the human structure, creating fractal patterns which effectively conceal a man from himself.

More on Change and Transformation

It is not one's innermost self, not the abiding reality within each organism which is to be changed. What needs study is the relationship of oneself to the interplay of energies that make up the body/mind structure. What needs modifying is one's attitude toward the manifold aspects of one's existence which are largely the reflection of passing thoughts and feelings.

Change begins with seeing the state of one's body, tension-filled or tension-free; with seeing one's vagrant associations and reactions; and with the hard-won capacity to maintain the priority of that which sees. In rare moments, the seeing itself prepares the way for a relationships between man and the higher forces to which he is, ordinarily, closed.

Transformation begins with an experience of unification and freedom where we understand more clearly and directly the reasons why we are here on earth. At this very moment the gate is either open or shut to an ever-present force. From this viewpoint, the commonplace 'how are you' takes on life-in-death import. Respond and test from an immediate immersion in this time/space moment.

Moods, movements,
Thoughts and feelings
Ever shifting
Inner patterns
Reflect still
Other inner
Chemical-genetic interacts
Present here
At this moment.
Behind the
Series of events
Which I
Call Me

What is my own?

World of impressions
Potential power
Awaits to illuminate

You.

Attention on
Subject you
Object, too.
At moment
Of receiving impressions
Acts as catalyst
Connecting inner and outer.

Duration and depth
At moment
You receive
Any impression
Greater its power
To nourish.

Impressions develop,
Transform into
Units of energy
Which affect others
Centuries later.

Listen to the poet's words
Look at Rembrandt's portrait.

Stop—wait.
Stop—again.

Consciously receiving
The smallest impression
Is step toward
New relationships.

To open doors,
Subconscious levels
Mute, not capable
Of direct communication
Need you.

We see, touch, taste
Hear, smell, feel.
Each moment
Each impression
Acted upon
By previous impressions
Like food
Is transformed.

Experiencing

Lovingly touch
The humblest object
This page.

Knowingly hold
A pencil.
Hear the silence.

Move to
Another part
And still another
Of body structure.
Let go
The neck
Shoulders, too.

Aware of
Right side
Then of left
Remain rooted
In lower torso.

Waiting gently
Attention receptive
Opening only
To this space/moment.
No past, no future
Breathe the moment.

Dispersed attention
Is suddenly collected
Adding further
Dimension to
Human existence.

Unifying, fusing
Bringing
Bliss-filled
Fullness of
Worlds inside
And out.

Reason/intuition
Abandoning neither
Integrate the one
With the absolute
The other with
The relative.

Reality.

Stillness heard
The treasure
Hidden
Is revealed.
Direct is
One's knowledge
Approachable, intelligible
The void.

Remaining aware
Of the Stillness

Plenitude.

Giving, receiving,
Transmitting, transforming,
Man's body mediates
Energies on every level.

Permeable, impressionable
Body/mind structure is
Made to transmute.

Intermediary between
Myriads of zones
The subtle complex
Which each one calls
I—Me—Myself
Like the sun
Renews itself
Each Day.

Process begins
With awareness.

Presence in present
With look at
Here/now state
This moment.

Silent listening
Reverberates and dissolves
Long-standing tensions,
Equilibrates, fine tunes
The interplay of energies.

Awareness
Not forced,
Not contrived.

A simple stop
Tension-free body
Tension-free mind
Tension-free breathing
Sensitively accepting

Wholeness.

"How, indeed, could it be possible for man, who is limited on six sides—by east, west, south, north, deep, and sky—to understand a matter which is above the skies, which is beneath the deep which stretches beyond the north and south, and which is present in every place, and fills all vacuity?"
—St. Gregory the Wonderworker
(c. 213-268)

The moment I die to myself, the moment I throw myself away, joy—even ecstasy—bursts through me. At this moment, I can say yes to everything I affirm as my existence. All the world is fine just as it is.

Ecstasy is an experience that is beyond verbal and intellectual comprehension, a glimpse of another existence and completely different from ordinary attitudes and viewpoints.

The onset of the ecstatic moment does not depend on, nor does it come from outside oneself. It is a call from the "purity in oneself," in St. Gregory's word; it is present everywhere and fills all vacuity. It is the same force which animates one's instinctive drives, one's associative thoughts. But it is a force which now takes another form.

How can one experience ecstasy without transcending oneself, without freeing oneself from the incessant domination of one's instinctive life? To go out of oneself, to be in touch with one's essential reality, is to hold in abeyance those forces which dominate one's existence.

Sometimes a sudden shock will bring a cessation of the associative processes, will intervene to free one from imprisonment by oneself.

But too often man is unable to disengage himself from himself. He is unable to move outside of the two-dimensional bondage of his twenty-four hour conditioning by society into the free world of joy and ecstasy. From the moment of his birth, an ersatz culture has chipped away at whatever spiritual dimension he may have possessed.

"Nirvana is where the two-fold passions have subsided and the two-fold hindrances are cleared away."
—Lankavatara Sutra

More on Thought

The Unknown cannot be captured, put on the table, defined and subjected to an intellectual analysis. But the Experience itself is not beyond our grasp.

What part does thought play in approaching this experience?

Some thoughts will help and others will be a barrier in seeking the experience of what I do not know. Just as collectively we face ecological disaster by disturbing the equilibrium of the earth, the individual faces disharmony whenever there is wrong functioning of mind.

Ideally thought should enable us to know the consequences of our actions—thought can even help us know the consequences of thought itself. It could function as a policeman, pointing out directions, keeping order in the community we call our body, helping to regulate the feelings, the other centers.

It is undeniable that the feeling of Mystery in oneself often comes when there is a cessation of ordinary thinking, when the mind is in free movement, not caught by any thing. When one has enough free attention to see and even choose one's associations, one learns a great deal from the experience. One may even accept that the eventual role of thought is to value it for its possibility to still itself.

Periods of stillness, of conscious direction of thought, are immensely valuable accumulators of the energy needed for the experience of the unknown.

New associations may never entirely cease, but they are vulnerable to interruption by a sudden shock or by a stop. To be able to hold the silence is a matter of the greatest import in making a leap into the unknown, where one lives and is in a different world, with new meaning and sensitivity presently unheard of.

THERE IS a middle ground, a basic Reality embracing self and Self. It may be called my true nature. To discover what prevents me from the experience of it, I have only to look at myself, just as I am.

It is so simple.
At this moment, what is my state? I let my attention embrace myself.

I am very still. I follow my breath. I watch the movement of thoughts and associations. Feelings become quiet. Activity in the head diminishes.

I remain very still, refusing the mind's inclination to reach for anything. Thoughts and feelings come and go like floating clouds. They are not me.

The experience is at one and the same time, both active and passive. Through sensation of the body, I perceive that I am. Yet, I do not know who or what I am. I am witness to my existence.

I am aware of a feeling, an accepting awareness. I am very still, relating to the silence that is both inside and outside.

Nothing is lacking at this moment.

There is another Reality
Ever present—

A world of subtle energies.
Obscured moment to moment
By thoughts and feelings
By movements that
Harmonize and clash.
Within man's structure
An ever-thickening web
Conceals a man from himself.

This network has its own life,
Its own momentum.
A shock, a flash
may demolish it
for an instant.
But the thick veil
Man calls his life
Quickly re-establishes itself.

Man's organism shelters
Many kingdoms, principalities
Which speak, assert, maintain
As if each were the whole.

Cut away from Self,
Ignorant of his Reality,
Man suffers and pleasures.

Transformation rests on
Reconciling self and Self.

Aware of Self
And these small usurpers
Cease their clamor.
Consciousness and nature
Begin to be served.

Consider this:
An image appears,
Storming the brain,
Producing a wave of angry reactions,
Poisoning the body-bloodstream,
Upsetting the brain equilibrium.

See the image from another place
Its energy flows back
Brings life to the seer.

When I stop and see
There is a change in tempo,
A new relating of
Heart, body and mind.
A potential link to
The Other,
To Self.
My part is to look
To welcome the seeing
With full knowing
With infinite sensitivity.

Seeing is the experience
The middle ground which points
Toward freedom.
Openness to what is here
Attention the every moment key.

In a quiet state
Knowledge firmly grounded,
Cognition of stillness transforms.

The way one sits, moves,
Breathes
Is the foundation
Creating the inner alignment
To receive another
Current of energy.

This energy needs me
And I share the need.
Here the pathway,
First body,
Then breath,
Then openness
Then the all
Of stillness.

We miss the mark
When we turn to anything
Or to anyone
Other than God/I/Reality.
Turning to an image or to
Concepts like God/I/Reality
We miss the mark.
Subtle is this turning
Eluding all
But the pure.

The unknown noumenal
Seldom contacted
Brings an energy
Which too infrequently
Enters daily existence.

Fused the two circles
Offer another vision.

Relating and interfacing
The two natures
Depend on man's
Being.
In his ordinary state
Of waking sleep
Man is cut away
From his potentiality.
Body/mind/feeling,
Ordinarily are too torpid
Or too agitated
Functioning at different tempos
They are unable
To understand each other.

The noumenal nature
Sometimes unveiled
Through shock or accident
Brings other levels of energy
Unexpected coherency and certitude.

Rarely do we see
The complete man
One who functions
From both natures
Who lives and plays
In both worlds
Reconciling and riding
The shifting tides.

We are modelled
As a system
That can observe itself.
Mind and body
Functioning coherently,
This is the way.
Convergence.

But reckon upon
Discrepancies:
A speeded-up mind tempo,
Bodily constrictions.
Distraction.

Mind wishes for unity,
For consciousness.
Can have this idea as an aim.
Mind can see the
Necessity of engaging
The whole self.
But it forgets
Does not know
How to enlist
Body/feeling cooperation.

Choiceless/awareness
Not forced or contrived
Inevitably harmonizes
Maintains equilibrium
Brings alignment of
Disparate energies.

Attention/awareness
Sensitizes body
Unveils the muffled
Voices of
Invisible chemistries.

In the middle ground
The meeting place of
being and Being.

An inner flow
Finds its way
And blends
With the world of form.
Livening, renewing
Bringing unification
Inexpressible meaning
To the smallest.
Beneficence touches
Each moment
With light.

We accept
A persona/ego
As 'myself,' as 'I'.

Challenge/change this
As the master does
Bring 'the other'
To the word
To the form
To the smallest gesture.

Outward active
Inwardly stillness
Reflects itself
In every transaction.

The secret?
In the activity
Attend to the quiet.
In the silence
Attend to the form.

Listen to the stillness
To the order within
Always present
Not divorced
Not in opposition
To movement.

A master is distinguished
By his ability
To be inwardly still
While moving,
Inwardly active
While doing nothing
Full engaged
Without attachment.

Active/passive
Is experienced
As a polar tension.
In music
The pauses between the sounds.
In painting
The spaces between the forms.

The timeless element
And the time bound

Are not alien
One to the other.
Every Man's true nature
Is rooted in beauty and ease.
Realize this
And be immersed
In the joy that
We are so painfully
Seeking.

The Bliss Meditation

God be in my breath
God be in my head
God be in my body
God be in my arms
God be in my legs
God be in me
God be all around me

God be in my eyes.
God be in my mouth
God be in my tongue
God by in my saliva
God be in my breath
God be in me
God be all around me

God be in all.
God be in No Thing.
God be.

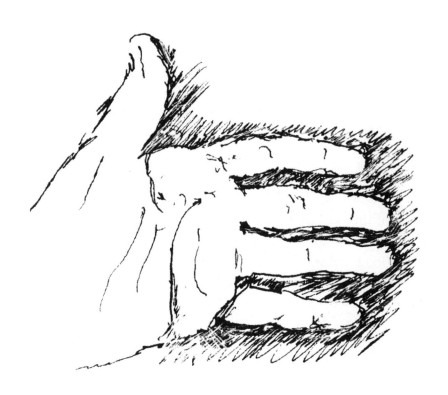

I look at myself sitting here. I am aware of the body that sits here. I see the breathing–how the breath comes and goes. I see the tension, the relaxation in different parts of my body.

I begin to be aware of immense silence. All my attention is concentrated on the stillness. My breathing anchors me here. I am more sensitive to this moment, this moment which comes to me pure, without the intrusion of thought.

The stillness begins to help me.

Breathing is quiet. Body begins to relax. The mind is freer. If thoughts come, I simply watch. A new level of letting go, of opening, of being here, listening…listening to the silence…this moment of silence.

I try to go deeper, but the trying is not a trying. It is surrendering to the moment. Always, always I can return to the breathing.

Now, in the stillness, I begin to be aware of a relation with another reality.

IV
CONVERSATIONS

with a Tibetan Master, Chatral Rinpoche
with Dorothea Dooling
with David Appelbaum

A NUMBER OF extraordinary conversations with Tibetan Masters were recorded in India in 1971. These tapes were made by William Segal in a year that saw ten million refugees in cholera-ridden camps around Calcutta in the Fall, and ended with the brief Indo-Pak war that created an independent Bangladesh from what had been East Pakistan.

When first heard, the tapes were deemed undecipherable. A tremendous amount of background sound and numerous breaks in the reels resulted in a far from complete transcription. With the help of modern technology, the conversations finally emerge. What remains—beyond the language, the ideas and the voice quality—are subtleties that preserve the flavor of the dialogues and the thought of the masters.

When Mr. Segal came to Delhi in May, it was already as hot as India gets before the monsoon brings some relief in June-July. I had arranged in advance for him to meet the Dalai Lama at His Holiness' residence at Dharamsala, in the hills northwest of Delhi. That involved an overnight journey by train and then a difficult jeep ride over mountain roads. Traveling light as always, William Segal set forth, accompanied by Lobsang Lhalungpa as interpreter and guide, not only to overcome any language barriers but to interpret a teaching and a culture that he knew so well, as son of the last State Oracle of Tibet, and as a personal friend of His Holiness.

As it turned out, interpreters were needed only at the beginning of the interview, as the Dalai Lama soon warmed to the occasion and broke into English. A more direct exchange ensued. Evidently Lhalungpa had told His Holiness that William Segal was familiar with Zen Buddhism, and at one point the Dalai Lama explained with gestures that the robe of Zen reached only to the knees, but that of Tibetan Buddhism covered everything, right down to the feet.

It was on a second trip several months later in November that the exchanges with Dudjom Rinpoche, the head of the Nyingmapa school of Tibetan Buddhism, and with Chatral Rinpoche, another respected Nyingma lama, took place in the hills around Darjeeling, north of Calcutta. In addition to seeing Dudjom Rinpoche and Chatral Rinpoche, there were visits to Kanjur Rinpoche and Gyurtala Rinpoche.

As nearly as we can now know, Chatral's reference to Gurdjieff's stint of two or three years in a Tibetan monastery at the beginning of this century has historical validity. My best guess is that Mr. Gurdjieff was thoroughly familiar with Dzogchen practices, as transmitted by the Nyingmapa lamas. In any case, the sole tape transcribed in its entirety was the conversation with Chatral Rinpoche, which we believe will be of great interest to those men and women who try to follow a path of awareness, of presence in the moment, now.

—J. GEORGE

A Conversation with Chatral Rinpoche

The meeting with Chatral Rinpoche, known as the "Tiger" Rinpoche, was held in a monastery located in a mountainous sector, near Darjeeling. One of Chatral's disciples took part in the answering, as well as carrying the task of translating.

Translator: Ah, you know, Rinpoche wants to know about your background, your spiritual practice that you have done so far. Particularly were you initiated by any other great teachers or were you self-developed or was the man who?... If he does not know your background, it is difficult for him to speak very frankly.

WS: I understand. *(Here, Segal speaks of his relationship to Ouspensky during the 1941–46 period in America, and to Gurdjieff in 1947–49. He also speaks about his friendship with Daisetz Suzuki, 1950-66.)* Can you tell about training or esoteric centers in Tibet?

CR: Your question is about the Swat Valley in Pakistan, which was center of Tantra practice? Your question concerns complete solitude? Because we mentioned a Sufi monastery in Pakistan and there is a description of this Tibetan lama by the name of Dnujembe, the Swat Valley was the important spiritual center from which many teachers came.

WS: When did they visit it, in what period?

CR: In various periods... thirteenth...twelve, thirteenth century, I think.

WS: Do you think this monastery still exists?

CR: No. This monastery, this center was Tantric, for Tantric practice; most of the devotees attained enlightenment. And so you have only the ruins, nothing left. There is also a very great stupa which contained many of the favorite writings on esoteric teachings and also relics.

WS: I see.

CR: Because in some way, this is, according to some of our own writings… this center was part of India — in the old days, when they had certain territory extended far beyond present borders. And in the case of Tibet, Tibet had a very great, extensive territories under its, you know, domination. But then, due to historical developments and, ah, the decline in the power of central authority, Tibet was divided into many little principalities and each one ruled by chieftains. So maybe this was the case with India, because foreigners came and they ruled and divided the country and, you know, then the territory sort of started shrinking. So perhaps the Pakistan then was, you know, part of India.

WS: Were there descriptions of special methods, training or teaching methods, in this monastery?

CR: This Swat Valley was certainly an important esoteric center and, according to our literary sources, somewhere near there was a great teacher, Padmasambhava. And so there was a good deal of spiritual activities propagating teachings. Even earlier, this was an important center during the lifetime of Buddha. While in India, Buddha propagated the teachings conducive to the temperamental need of people. These were mainly exoteric teachings. And then, in this Swat Valley, there was a king called Endabuddhi at the time of Buddha, and he wanted a very special teaching which he could practice without giving up any of his worldly ties, worldly pursuits. Therefore, our Buddha found that the king was now ripe for receiving esoteric teachings. Thereupon, Lord Buddha gave him one of the highest teachings, giving him the initiation, and also instructions, about the practice. And a number of others got initiations and, ah, they then followed the teachings, practiced, and most of them in their lifetime got enlightenment — the enlightenment not only of the spiritual but even the physical. All of them obtained their radiant forms, and all of them taking their radiant forms. The whole place was filled with great yogins.

WS: Yes.

CR: So this was important center. Once the devotees attained their enlightenment, they left no earthly remains. They were all attained, both physically and spiritually. And, ah, then there were a good many Tibetan masters who either physically visited this sacred place, or in their spiritual form, in meditative trance, they spiritually visited this place. Some of them had the power to visit spiritually; while still in their sleep they visited sacred places. These things indeed happened like that.

WS: Yes. Now, the whole problem is to carry one's remembering into life. In other words, while doing everything that one does in the city, to be the same as if one were in a monastery; this is a question on which I would like your views.

CR: We have been receiving many letters from the West and all of them, young people or old people, they all are anxious to get the teachings for meditation. Now, in our own tradition, we had great many seers and teachers who had such tremendous power to read the minds of their disciples and potential disciples, that they could foresee the potential nature of each individual, each disciple. And accordingly, they could give each person teachings, maybe even just three sentences, and he would find his enlightenment. Because in such case, there was, you know, the quality of teacher, the standard of the teachers was very great.

Secondly, the requisite qualities of disciples, the inner urge for spiritual practice, for spiritual attainment, their devotion, their determination, and, ah, all these were there. In addition, the teachings that were suitable were also readily available from these great teachers. When these factors were present, there was no problem that any individual would gain his enlightenment without difficulty. And this was the case because in each case, the disciple meets his teacher and the teacher would at once know that this was his disciple, that his destiny was to attain his spiritual perfection.

WS: ...and today?

CR: This does not exist at present moment. We are living in the age of moral, mental, and spiritual crises—all kinds of conflicts and crises. Therefore, men like me cannot claim to have the spiritual power which would easily read the inner capacities of prospective individuals or disciples.

Therefore, for us, it is much safer to follow the path laid down by the great teachers. That is, to follow everything according to the various teachings. That is, that once a disciple is anxious to get teachings, he must find time to devote himself to his practice and to go to this teachers and get this, receive the teachings. And he must know how he should really proceed in this practice. This, with his teacher, the relationship between the two — both are very important. Therefore, once this is done, then he does not straight away meditate because the teaching given is according to his own capacity. And therefore, step by step, he is given teachings and, ah, teachings certainly are not just one simple thing. First of all, an ordinary man must first observe, he must study the nature of existence itself, which is all impermanent, undergoing always changes…tremendous changes…nothing remains stable, nothing remains constant. Therefore, including his own physical body, and even his thoughts, everything undergoing changes.

Therefore, realizing this nature of things, he must also realize the nature of existence itself, which is so full of sufferings. And, having realized this, he must find a way out of this existence. Therefore, he has to develop strong determination to work for his liberation. And, ah, therefore he goes and he receive teachings…how to carry this practice. And, after that, the guru decides when to give him initiation, which is the most important beginning of his esoteric practice, which introduces him to esoteric practice, which is not itself enough, he must have also teachings which explain the various aspects of the practice, and, ah, with which he can carry on his practice.

Now, concerning this esoteric practice, as you have probably heard, there are, in esoteric tradition, different levels of Tantra, which is exclusive to our teachings, and which is actually divided into three parts.

WS: What is common to all four sects?

CR: These are four divisions of Tantras which are common to all. In the fourth stage, according to Nyingmapa, there is one higher division and this division of Tantra can be divided into three parts, three stages. But this is just by way of explanation. But this is not part of the, part of the answer to your question, but this is what I want to explain. And in these three divisions of highest form of esoteric teachings, the one is called Mahayoga, the second one is Anuyoga, the third one is Atiyoga. And, ah, the Atiyoga deals with the highest form of esoteric teachings. Therefore it is not a question of how an individual can follow all these different stages.

Now, in order to follow and receive higher teachings, you must really, you must practice certain fundamental teachings which bring about necessary qualities within one's own mind. In other words, make himself ripe to receive high initiations, high teachings. Without preparation, practice, the teaching will not help.

WS: That's understandable. Yes.

CR: And so, in order to receive high initiations, higher esoteric practice, it is necessary to overcome the barriers — emotional, intellectual—he does certain preliminary exercises. Going through these various stages, he develops greater and greater urge and determination. And, at the same time, prepares himself for doing higher practice. So that when he completes this, he receives the higher initiation.

WS: That's the same in almost every teaching, isn't it?

CR: Well, in the Tibetan Buddhist tradition, when we talk about tradition, there is always emphasis on the need, first of all, to concentrate on the mind, the nature of mind. Whether one talks about philosophy, doctrine, either way ultimately, everything comes to this point: dealing with the mind. There are other schools like Mahamudra which also deal under various different terms with the same thing — all concerning the mind: how men should understand it, should handle it, tackle it, develop it. All this comes to the same thing, it is same thing.

Therefore, as far as the West is concerned, especially America, which is very, very materially advanced country with all your science and technology, which has reached such a tremendous scale of development, that you can now send men and men can land on the moon, and even perhaps you could go higher and higher. But, spiritually speaking, all these are creation of mind. And you have done so much in the field of tackling… *(Conversation breaks.)*

(Translator speaks with admiration of American and Russian outer space achievements, but at the same time indicates that Tibet's achievements in "going inward" were equally important. Later, he again refers to the moon landing.)

CR: …but no matter what tradition, no one has ever attained awakening or enlightenment simply by reading scriptures. We have so many great masters through the history who all received the teachings from their teachers, teachers who had attained their enlightenment. There are great maharishis, great teachers who had displayed their miraculous powers.

But there are equally large number of teachers who did not display such miraculous powers. But it doesn't mean that those who displayed miraculous powers had greater awakening or greater spiritual power than those who did not. In all cases, they had almost equal understanding and had equal awakening.

Now, when you talk about many other religions, there is always the feeling among the followers that his religion is the best. And all others are not as good as their own. This applies to Christianity, because Christians perhaps believe theirs is the only way. So does Hindu or even the Muslim. And this is because he has faith in his own religion.

Now if you think that faith is the right thing, then faith has different categories or different kinds of faiths. For instance, people who believe in the doctrine of Communism, they also have faith in Communism. Or people who believe in tenet that is totally opposed to Communism they also have faith in this. Even as we Buddhists, we believe that the teachings of Buddhism are the best for understanding and reaching the highest goal of man. And even in our own teachings, there are various methods expounded by different teachers whose particular interpretation of the teachings of Buddha concerning truth become different schools of thought and tradition. But our ultimate goal is to reach enlightenment.

That does not mean that we should only concentrate on this highest aspect without going through various stages of practice. Because only in cases of very few individuals is it possible for him to receive teachings in terms of few words and reach awakened state within a matter of a very short time. We had one such as... there are many, many who actually had attained spiritual enlightenment in a matter of just short time, but, nowadays, it is very difficult to reach such a stage without much effort. For instance, we had one teacher who was very young, in fact, he was a child. And he lived only up to the thirteen years of his age. And from his fifth year, he started learning teachings, taking teachings, and within a matter of just short perid, a few years, he not only mastered the teachings—understood, got initiated, practiced, and attained enlightenment—and not only he attained enlightenment, but he also started propagating the Dharma. Therefore, in matter of just few years, he did everythng...ah, but perhaps we have to spend so many years, maybe many lives.

Therefore, according to the individual potentialities and capacities, some can attain enlightenment within a matter of a very short time. Others may not attain it at all in this life. But, as we talk about teachings, the ultimate goal is certainly our understanding, our efforts to understand the ultimate nature of things, the nature of mind.

But there are various other methods...for some minds, there is the devotional way, so that they reach a certain level of understanding and, in the process, they cultivate certain qualities and, therefore, they become ripe for receiving the higher teachings.

In some cases, some of the masters say, whatever you do physically or mentally, all these are just means to deceive yourself if you cannot just devote yourself to what is the ultimate practice, the most essential practice. This does not mean that everybody should follow and do the same thing. Milarepa, whose life was translated into English, has become well-known among the Western people. But we have had great many teachers like him, whose lives, whose teachings, have not been translated and made known to others.

For us, now it is to concentrate on the teachings according to one's teachers and traditions and, in our case, it is a matter to be taken very carefully. For instance, no one can simply read a text and meditate and attain. He has to look for a teacher, a guru, with all the qualities necessary for leading the disciple. Not only learning, not only the mastery of the scriptures, but also human qualities, the understanding, the warmth, the feeling, the compassion. Not only this, but also the inner quality, capacity and power, spiritual attainment. All these are necessary.

And on the part of the disciple himself, he must have deep spiritual urge for receiving teachings, for carrying on this inner practice. One is given certain initiation in which he is introduced to the nature of things, the nature of mind, and with this understanding, he gets more and, ah, instructions and therefore, he carries on his practice. It is just like your American scientists who have developed technology which made it possible for your people to fly and land on the moon. The practice can be compared with this same thing, because it is a journey from this existence to the beyond.

The Buddhas and great teachers are like the ones who landed on the moon, who traveled through this, who had the experience, who knew the techniques, the methods, who knew the conditions and everything. And, therefore, when they came back, they told their disciples... *"if anyone wishes to visit the planets, this is the way."* There are always obstacles, barriers. How to overcome these barriers? And this is what actually the teachings are.

(Conversation resumes after a short break.)

CR: Everything depends on the man — if he knows, if he has practiced, if he has understood. If he has reached certain stage of spiritual development, then there is no reason why he cannot propagate and make teachings available to others. Otherwise, he will be just like a blind leading another blind.

(Here the conversation touches on the Gurdjieff teaching. Chatral Rinpoche indicates that Gurdjieff himself received training at a Tibetan monastery in the Swat Valley referred to earlier in the tape.)

CR: In the teachings of Buddha, one of the most important factors is the development of mind. Whatever practice one follows, ultimately the practice must produce its own results in terms of reducing mental deficiencies, and in eliminating the defilements, the ignorance, the hatred, the lust, and all the prejudices and mental deficiencies. And, at the same time, development of human qualities... the sympathy, the compassion. And also sharpening of understanding, enlarging the intelligence in comprehending higher and more profound teachings. If these things are the results of the practice of meditation, then one's meditation is really making good progress. It's producing good results. If, on the other hand, these qualities or results are not achieved, then meditation has no meaning at all. It has not produced good result. Therefore, on the one hand, we think always in terms of the elimination of defects, deficiencies of the mind; on the other, the development of qualities. And, if these two results are there, then the practice is all right, the practice is good.

WS: Our teaching is in accord with yours.

Translator: We are in agreement with you. We can understand whether a disciple has the understanding of the transmission that was given to him. He is, for instance, given a particular instruction to carry on in his meditation, and he is told that, by doing this, he will go through stages of experiences. And, once he does this, he comes and gives us his experience. And if his experience tallies with what we have already described, then he has reached a definite understanding. But then there are others who carry on the practice, but still cannot reach that level of understanding. Because this we know by exchange of ideas, exchange of experiences. So it is not difficult at all.

CR: In the Vajrayana tradition, guru gives certain instructions concerning the meditation, designed to make one understand the true nature of mind. And then disciple goes away and does meditation in solitude. After certain time, he comes back and relates his experiences to his guru. And if guru finds that he has reached definite understanding, then he gets more instructions, so that he can carry on to stabilize the gain he has already made. But if he does not reach that stage, he is again asked to go back and repeat the same practice. And there are people who have more, sort of, inner capacity to reach and understand quickly. And others, in spite of their repeated attempts, still cannot come to the same position.

WS: That's very understandable.

CR: Well, that is what I repeat in the very beginning. You know, all the traditions, there are various methods, various ways of making the disciple to reach the level of awakening and understanding. For instance, we had great masters like Tilopa who did not give teachings to his disciple Naropa so easily without making him to go through twenty-four sacrifices, personal sacrifices — twelve major ones and twelve minor ones — each involving tremendous physical, mental hardship. And after all this, then Naropa was found ready. One day Tilopa beat him almost to death. And when Naropa fell unconscious, he woke up from that state of unconsciousness and, thereupon, he found himself in fully awakened state, which was no different from anything that was attained by Buddha or any great master.

In our own time, there are teachers who can see a disciple's mental qualities, mental capacities, potentialities. In each case, the teacher only gives him so much teachings, just enough for breaking open awakening. But we don't possess the great qualities of the great teachers. Therefore, our approach is, since we don't know the inner capacity of the man—capacity that is in a latent form, that has not been developed, that is lying hidden—therefore, we give them the more or less complete teachings so that any aspect of these teachings will help bring about the desired result.

WS: *(laughs)* Good.

CR: And, at the same time, if these complete teachings don't produce desired result, then we will give them what is known as instantaneous teachings.

WS: Which are... what are instantaneous teachings?

Translator: (interrupting) Ah, well, he has not explained, but this is something that needs to be explained. Anyway, there are various methods where the disciple gets teachings in an unusual way... in other words, he receives teachings direct from the teachers, the great teachers of the past, who appear to him and give him the teachings directly.

WS: And his idea about everything being a dream...that we live in a dream and take the dream for the reality?

CR: All things convert in our Buddhist tradition to, for instance, mirage...

WS: Ah, yes.

CR: ...dream, illusion, and, ah, having no entity or nature of their own. Everything like a dream. For instance, when you dream at night a huge, vicious tiger approaching you and trying to attack you and, ah, eat you up. You experience this in your dream, that you had experience, sensation of seeing the tiger and also the fear that he might certainly attack and harm you. When you get up the next morning, it was just a bad dream... it had not existence of its own, no reality of its own. Similarly, the fact that you and I meet here... is a dream.

WS: *(laughs)* You would say that?

CR: ...not more than a dream. We take it to be real... neither I nor you, in our sleep, take the dream to be false, as having no reality of its own. But we don't take life to be false, to be illusory. We take it to be real. We always hold onto it as real. Because of this grasping or holding to the sensations, to cognizance, taking as real — which is illusion, which is not real — in actual life we are so overcome by delusions that we don't see the reality. Because we are incapable of seeing things as they truly are... which is nothing.

WS: *(laughs)* Very good. Very fine.

Teachers and Teachings
Students and practice
step by step
the way is wended.

Each Individual
unique, Universal.

Inborn capacities
advance understanding
inborn lacks
awakens to sleep-states
together reveal
impermanence, eternities.

Teacher and techniques
not enough
knowledge and study
not enough
meditations, exploration
not enough

Warmth and compassion
also needed.

Mind must Know
The nature of mind
mind must know
assertions of mind
must know
assertions of feelings
of body sensation.

Must know that
human nature
is both
ultimate and relative.
In front
mind looks to
is drawn entirely
to objects,
to things, to surfaces.
Looking behind
in background of you
in core
of your being
absence of objects
absence of language
presence of something
Beyond.

Existence—
Silence is always and everywhere.

Silence, Clarity
Just where you are
searchingly, wholly
go toward the moment
this tremendous new moment
no you, no not you
the pure point
everywhere, always.

Go further where
there is nowhere,
no-one,
no coming, no going
no place knowable
the place where
you are now.

In the nearness
the Silence surrounds
beckons the burdened body
soothing the errant mind
freeing the heart.

Beyond body and mind
transcending all the Silence.
But can the Silence know itself?
Its undreamed necessities?

It is through the body that sits here
that I go to my true nature.

A Conversation with Dorothea Dooling

This conversation with Dorothea (Doro) Dooling, founding editor of Parabola magazine, took place in New York in the fall of 1988.

Doro Dooling: You know, the funny thing about every issue of PARABOLA, every theme we pick, is that we always end up questioning the very words we've chosen. And "Questions" is no exception. We had to come to the *question* of questions, in order to examine it from a number of different angles.

William Segal: The fundamental question, of course, is "Who am I?" This is a query which comes out of the very fact of life. And because life confronts us with so many trials, so many sufferings — and so many joys — we begin to ponder, "What's it all about?" And always, in every era, a small percentage of humanity pursues these questions: "Who am I, essentially? How do I liberate myself? What is reality?" My own personal question began when as a young publisher, I was walking down the street one day to my office and I suddenly stopped and said to myself, "What on earth am I doing? What is all this for?" Many men come to that point in life. And at this moment, a man—or a woman—senses that there is something within himself which can change the equation of being. He has that moment of "Oh, ah, something's *here*." And at that moment, a door opens. He may or may not continue further. The chances are that the pull of gravity will close the door and he will be shut away from his ever-present possibility.

DD: But I think when a real question comes up in one's life, it has a way of attracting some kind of force of another level. It attracts a teacher. They say that "when the pupil is ready, the master appears."

WS: It seems to work that way, although one cannot see it clearly. In the presence of a man or woman of being, there is a real question, in the sense that you are stunned, you are shocked into a silence, where the ordinary machinations of the mind don't help you. It brings you face to face with your original nature, your original face. And what is this strange question that this person of being presents? It's a glimpse of another reality which is always here, ready to step into the equation of our relationships.

DD: But it's an unknown, isn't it?

WS: It's both unknown and known. It's here, but I can't put it on the table and dissect it. But it's here. It's as concrete or as liquid as this cup of coffee.

DD: There certainly is a way of questioning that can lead to this unknown known—toward a dimension in life, a new openness. But isn't there also a way of asking questions—of struggling—which keeps me from this other reality? Which blocks the other reality by insisting on answers, solutions? I was thinking of an experience I had a long time ago A young cleric came to visit me one day at my home. He had heard something about various things that I was interested in and he said, "Oh, yes, I think you have an entirely different set of answers from mine." And I had a sudden strong, very negative reaction to this remark, and I think it was really the first time I ever thought about the question of questions. Because when I faced this hot reaction, I realized that those who have taught me anything, or helped me in any way, have never given me answers; they only helped me to deepen my questions. And the idea of a "set of answers" is, in fact, the reason I left the church I was raised in. Churches have sets of answers — dogmas. And that to me is the degeneration of search, not the way toward that reality that you were speaking about. It's the way away from it. Now maybe that's too downright!

WS: Well, I would put it that an event can be experienced at many levels. And maybe at one level, the kind of assurance in the form of an answer might help the search. I agree with you that a verbal answer is not the ultimate answer. The ultimate answer is that there is no answer—no answer in the sense that it is an experience which cannot be put in words or formulated. But at the same time there are many ways, and for me the most efficacious way is to be told to stop, to be aware that I am unaware of an ever-present stillness underneath the activity of my life. This is a direction which I respect; it can be validated by one's own effort. And in a way this is an answer which is given by different disciplines and religions. There is the Judeo-Christian "Be still and know that I Am." Zen Buddhism gives the enigmatical "mind and body dropped" answer. Tribal primitive religious often come to stillness of the mind through physical movement, dancing. Some shamans work through drugs. It is, eventually, a new understanding of who we are. Free from our head associations, one may evaluate freshly. So that there is no activity of thinking about having an answer — or having a question.

DD: That is really the aim of the koan isn't it?

WS: The aim of the koan is to enable the pupil to resolve what the mind cannot resolve. There is the ability to be engaged very actively in life, but at the same time to be non-attached. One does what one does with full enthusiasm: I love to drink coffee, to paint, to dig a garden or chop wood. But can I be wholly in the act but not attached to it? And at the same time, be in relation to this "other," this stillness, which is in me, in you, in everything. This requires discipline, which one reaches through various methods. It's not only meditation, and it certainly isn't through scholastic studies or through prayer of the ordinary kind, although prayer can be a cessation of thought, a giving up, a letting go and being here totally. Now perhaps to be that way does require a great preliminary doing; I'm not sure about that. As an old man who has been through a lot of that sort of practice, I don't think it's really necessary. I don't see the sense of it now. I think if I were in the hands of a master today, he would simply tell me, "Look, mister, just be still. Watch your breathing. Get your center of gravity down here." And then this appears. This is in you, it's always here. All one has to do is open to it. So I don't see the sense of all these schools and all these disciplines. I do see the sense, because one is unable, one is not capable as one is, in ordinary life.

DD: Don't you think it's possible that certain things are necessary depending on one's age and stage of development? The seeker may start off young, and certainly inexperienced. It seems to me that one has to go through all these things, and then perhaps one comes to a point where they are no longer necessary. And yet, would one have gotten to where one is now without having gone through all that earlier training?

WS: Probably not. Maybe what you're saying can be answered this way: If someone has to ask whether or not an exercise is necessary, than it *is* necessary. But there comes a time when there's certitude.

DD: You have to come to that point.

WS: Some take longer than others. It's a question of levels, and people are different. It may take some people thirty years, some three.

DD: It takes most people a long time though, don't you think?

WS: Well, you know, Doro, I was thinking. I believe we're in a different era. I'm not so sure it should take thirty years.

DD: Everything is speeding up.

WS: And I think in a way it's a wonderful thing.

DD: But we don't belong to this era. It's a new era. We lived in another era, when it took a long time.

WS: That's right. Nowadays you see texts and ideas printed that were not easily available before — even PARABOLA prints certain indications, which can be of great help. Formerly it was hard to find that sort of direction for the beginning of a way. Now many ways and even opportunities are presented. Very few Americans attempted to live in Zen monasteries before World War II. Today, you can go there rather easily. There are texts printed that were never printed before, and there are many people who have experience who can give you good preliminary guidance. One may not easily find a master, but one can find plenty of competent guides. The Tibetans have flocked here, the Zens, and the other Buddhists. Sufi and other teachings are available.

DD: And yet, Bill, it seems to me that the idea of the necessity of levels is still not commonly acknowledged or understood. Not at all. And we've had all these wonderful texts, things that people would have given their eye teeth to have been allowed to see thirty years ago; anybody can go out today and can buy on the mass market. You can go to a drugstore and buy *The Bhagavad-Gita*, for instance.

WS: Well, the overabundance of texts may now be a handicap, that's true.

DD: They get all mixed up. When these sacred texts come to the drugstores or the supermarkets, where anybody can read them, it seems to be that you have the leveling of levels, the annihilation of levels; everything gets flattened out. This is really the tendency of the new era that frightens me for the young people.

WS: I don't think there's anything to be frightened of. The reality is always here, even here in this room. One has to simply experience a moment of stillness. There it is.

DD: I believe in process, you see, and it can take you down as well as up. And question can come from above or below. There is the question that is implicit in search for the seeker reaching for a new reality: "Who am I? Where am I? Why am I?" And then there is the question which comes from above: the questions that the seeker is asked, sometimes by life, sometimes by the teacher, sometimes by God. The kind of questions that God asked Job, for instance. God knew the answer. He wasn't asking in order to find out something. He wasn't in front of the unknown. And the teacher asks the pupil questions, not because he's looking for something he doesn't know, but perhaps this is his way of calling up something in the pupil. So, do you see what I mean by these two directions that questioning takes?

WS: There are questions which can do away with the mechanical operation of the head. There are questions which cannot be answered by an accumulated bundle of knowledge. Unless there is this clearing of a ground for the emerging of the relationship with another force, questions and answers will go on *ad infinitum*. And there will only be more learning, more accumulation. But that's all right. The question is how to be in order to allow the relationship to take place — how to be open to another thought, another feeling. Without awakening to Self, the fact of thinking about something, objectifying something, obscures the ever-present relationship between the phenomenal and the noumenal. So this idea of questions coming from above or below is simply again, for me, preliminary.

DD: Of course, I'm not speaking about questions as if all questions were formulated in words. I'm thinking of the question of everybody's search, everybody's presence in front of something we don't know. So when I don't know, this is a question.

WS: Again, but in front of that, you are stopped. The question ceases, it falls away.

DD: The whole thing is to get the question out of the mental part and into being. Now, where do you ask the real question, the question that doesn't have any words, the question that is just an opening? Where does it come from?

WS: There you're up against the same thing. It has no words. One can't describe from where it comes. There are people who have tried to give it a name. The Void. The Emptiness. God. The Absolute. No-Thing. The Stillness. The Smile. The Flower. All these things are no-things.

DD: But that is what one is in front of.

WS: But once again, if you're asking a question, it's coming from the head. If you just try to be still — take a deep breath — sink down, sink; let it go: all of his dropping off reveals that there is no question, and there is no thing. And immediately it starts up again.

DD: What then is question? Is it a lack?

WS: That's the answer. Question, to me is openness. An openness, which contains everything, and there is an awakeness, there is a new way of living. Of being awake.

DD: We're trying to speak of something that can't be put into words and we have nothing but words to use. That's the difficulty we find ourselves in. But I agree that it's only when I give up all questions and answers I give up trying to *ask* questions, or to *find* answers, that I know that I am myself the question in front of the ultimate answer.

WS: Many people have tried to coin the right word. And there are many words which approximate the fundamental reality: Being. Absolute. True Self. Stillness. Words are quite different when they're spoken, when they're heard. How do we get beyond that? One time I saw someone tried to do it in print. At the bottom of the text was written, "Try to be still and hold your attention when you turn the page." If someone has enough experience and is willing to try that, he might find something. But many great people have tried to put it into words.

DD: All the great teachers used words.

WS: But there again, though all of the great teachers have used words, when those words are written on paper, they're quite different from when those great teachers spoke the words.

This fundamental reality comes through the teacher's spoken words, and once in a while the echo may come through the printed word, but very little of it. We're faced with a very difficult task, which only the great artists are able to solve. Rembrandt paints his picture, Mozart composes music, Shakespeare writes a play, and they bring you to the mystery, where words don't really matter. The concept keeps intruding and spoiling things. We're so busy up here, in the head — we're so busy with the ten-thousand things that we don't hear what's shouting at us.

DD: But there has to be a very strong and rigorous process of questioning before one can come to the point of passing beyond it.

WS: Well, I would put it that the questioning should be related to attention. To cultivate the habit of attentiveness is all-important. This could be the preliminary to relating to the ultimate principle in oneself. The capacity to be here whole-heartedly — that is the process of training that I would recommend.

DD: It does seem to me that there is a process of questioning that leads you to a place where you can meet this ultimate question.

WS: Well, that may be a pedagogical and historical situation—

DD: No, a personal one. When we began to try to make sense of our lives, weren't our first questions things like, Why do I behave like this? Or why can't I do what I think I'm going to do, what I've told myself I'm going to do? Why is it our first questions about our identity begin with our behavior? And yet later we come to the point where our behavior no longer matters to us so much, our questions about ourselves are much more interior. Identity isn't dependent on behavior. But it's a process, and I think it's a beautiful process. Where would we be without that ladder? If one is really attentive, as you say, to one's real questions, one can have confidence in the process. One can trust it.

WS: You speak of it as a process, Doro, whereas I would say that one could simply follow the dictum of "Know thyself," which means I'd like to know the operation of this mechanism. I should certainly try to find out all I can about the laws which dictate my well-being: physical, mental, and psychical. I certainly should know the laws of maintaining my earth, my physical self. I should know as much as possible about how to meet the demands of the society around me. I should know the so-called moralities. I should have as much knowledge as possible. But all of that fades away in relation to the other. And when you're at that level, then you can let it all go.

DD: But you have to climb up to that level.

WS: There comes a point where unless you meet someone — unless you experience the moment of a contact with a man of another level, or unless God or grace strikes you and you can add two and two together, all of this knowledge is useless— at any rate, in relation to what we are speaking about.

DD: But then there is process?

WS: I suppose yes, there is process. But at the same time, the reality is beyond space, beyond time. You can't say that it's this or that, or that it's long or short, or that it's timeless or in time. It *is*. Primary energy is in the cup of coffee, in you, in me, in everything. We're all in it. So when you say process, I say, yes, but can we not just open to it? It's here.

A Conversation with David Appelbaum

The following conversation with David Appelbaum, editor of Parabola, took place in New York in 1995.

David Appelbaum: What beckons you to study human speech?

William Segal: There are two aspects which are most interesting. The first is the power of the word when it is based on a special and mysterious energy which initially gave rise to the word. One says something, and, depending on the energy behind it, the word or sentence arouses or fails to evoke a corresponding energy in the listener. We all know that the same idea in the same words expressed by different people can have quite different impact. Searching for the key to this, it seems that the most important influence behind language is invisible, an invisible energy. From that point of view, a word or a sentence when spoken with attention, is charged with a special energy. Energy follows attention—where I put my attention there follows a flow of force—and where there's an inner presence accompanying what is expressed, power is added to whatever is spoken.

The other aspect which is interesting is the unique human capacity to poeticize language. Why does one combination of words make impact, stir interest or movement, while the same words in different combination fall flat? Poetry plays with words, makes them reverberate.

DA: That capacity is what interests me; when I feel the life of language and in feeling that, feel my own life again. How does one come to this capacity? Is it a gift, or is it a matter of practice?

WS: Some people have this extraordinary gift; their words and combinations of words have an effect that is greater than the average person's. Some are able to develop it. Certainly it must be like any other art of craft; practice and study and knowledge bring a heightened capacity to make words sing. Other people come to that place where their words ring true, have real meaning because of who they are. It comes back to what I said before—there must be an inner energy behind it, an inner emotional or intellectual quality. It is true, too, that people are gifted in different degrees in illuminating language, just as they are gifted in different degrees in relation to painting or carpentry or music.

DA: Sometimes it seems that language, almost on its own, has this power of suddenly throwing open the doors to a reality that's hidden. Is that a forgotten aspect of language? How would you understand that?

WS: There are very few occasions where we speak from the reality of the moment. If I spoke from this moment, there would be a concentration of energy that would make the moment alive. Each word would be underlined and would make the moment alive. And, depending on my capacity to feel as well as to bring thought to the words themselves, our communicating would have extra quality. Of course, the order of the words, the right words at the right time are weightier than language used in any old way.

DA: What is there in language itself that allows me to speak or try to speak from the reality of this moment?

WS: There are moments when we wish to relate to one another from the core of our being. Just talking, just exchanging comments is not enough. Still, language is our human mode, the major mode of expression. But language is a two-edged sword—it can serve reality or hide it. Take words like patriotism, love, duty…I can raise my hand and convey something to you through a gesture. Or I can say "Aum," and that sound may mean something to you. But to explain or develop a sentiment or a thought, I need suitable and expressive words, and the way one places the words, the choice of words—their novelty or unexpectedness—help to catch your interest. Your interest aroused, you're a little more awake to what's being said. That means there's more attention being paid on your part as well as mine—more participation of more parts of ourselves—and as interest develops, images in one's head begin to build further images; additional sources of energy develop. A continual energy creation is going on.

DA: So there's something in language that, for instance, now helps you and me relate in this very subtle kind of connection. I feel in some ways the words are an essential part of my exploring how to remain related to others.
WS: Language, like music, is one more key to unlock areas in the human psyche that would otherwise remain shut. If what I say interests you, you begin to open up different parts of you that are ordinarily closed. One part being opened is a key to another part being opened. So a few words, a few phrases spoken, unlocking a center in yourself, give rise to a whole series of door openings. One discovers something that has been in hiding. All this makes for new relationships. We relate

to each other through the way we express ourselves and language is a quintessential mode of expression.

DA: It seems as though many of my discoveries about myself, about the world, are discovered in language: "This is what this means." Is language something alive, something that expands as my awareness develops?

WS: Depending on how it is used, language is more or less alive. Compare dead language falling on deaf ears to language that touches the thought, opens up the thinking and feeling part. Words can touch feelings, and can even touch our senses by richness of texture. In the hands of a writer or poet, language reaches one or more parts of the mind/body configuration. Depending on the word itself, depending on how it is spoken, its sound—it can open up more or fewer passages…can bring an unexpected flowing-outward or emergence of energy which ordinarily is absent. If we speak only in clichés, as we do most of the time, it's not very interesting. But sometimes one speaks the right word at the right time and evokes a corresponding opening or interest, which starts the flow of energy that makes life interesting.

DA: But can language—something that you say or something that I read—bring me back to an unknown part of myself that is changeless?

WS: Some images open the mind and the feelings so that we begin to glimpse unsuspected levels in ourselves. Overused, familiar words have little effect, relatively small power to awaken.

The unexpected word or phrase, the fluid combination or the combination which carries a unique or different thought, is more evocative than the ordinary cliché. Some words, like some phrases in music or color passages in a painting, have more effect than others. Intervals, the spacing between the words, or the rhythm, the cadences, the relationship—they all play their part.

DA: The tempo, the timing. Even the printed page when it's read is read in time.

WS: [*quoting from a fourteenth-century Italian poem*] *"Out from its flying cage flies the nightingale."* An ordinary writer might have said, *"The nightingale flew out of its flying cage."* What a difference! [*He goes on*] *"And in tears he said, who opened its doors?"* [*emphasis on the "o" sounds*] The sound gives an extra dimension to the words themselves. So it must be that a true, whole art is one which touches more than one part, more than the intellectual part. One is not really able to intellectualize poetry.

DA: Do you think this art was once known by the poets of all cultures?

WS: It's still known in the sense that rhythms in music can be translated into words, and there are rhythms which enable one to control, to affect, to heal, to destroy. In literature, for instance, there is Coleridge's, "In *Xa*nadu did *Ku*bla *Khan* a *state*ly *plea*sure *dome* de*cree* [*emphasis on beats*] or the sonnets of Shakespeare. In our culture words have been so bandied about, so readily available, we fail to appreciate them. We don't live like the poets that we are. I think that in a more poetic age, I would relate to you differently, and we would talk in more poetical terms. We're surrounded by printed words, TV words, everybody talks too much (including myself, of course), and so we don't treasure this marvelous instrument of language.

DA: This interests me very much, the opening, expanding function of language, as well as the part that we know all too well—the dead language. But in this opening, is there a kind of intention? You've spoken of attention, but is there a kind of intention that is needed in order for me to speak in such a way that I invite you to open?

WS: There must be a threshold if language is to enter the human psyche. The threshold might be the space that precedes the uttering of the world. There can be a kind of calculated timing. But this has the danger of being a trick. A skilled actor, a Lawrence Olivier, uses his whole body as language, his whole bearing, as well as his lines. Still, insincerity and manipulation rarely deceive us.

DA: You mentioned Eckhart at the very beginning. When I read Eckhart, or when I hear of "that which is no thing," that seems to be a use of language which both says and unsays at the same moment. The trap of language seems to be that it leaves a kind of permanent trace—those words recorded in text—and the trap is that the fluidity, the movement is lost. In an approach to that which truly is unsayable, how do you use the place of language?

WS: We can't get away from the fact that language represents our thoughts and feelings. If the thought is a noble one or unusual one, if the feeling is genuine, it will find appropriate expression.

DA: And if you were struck by a sudden insight into reality, would there be words?

WS: I think that there would be a gasp, one would just say, "Oh," or simply an affirmation: "Yes." Something very simple. Insights into reality are hardly expressible through talk. Words would seem artificial and too cumbersome. Words, as wonderful as they are, are neither subtle nor swift enough to express very strong emotions. In fact, wouldn't a tremendously strong emotion paralyze speech?

DA: Would you say the same is true of deeper states of consciousness?

WS: No, because consciousness does not preclude awareness. There would be awareness in the sense of heightened cognition. The element of awareness itself implies more sensitive perception—a kind of calmness, a coolness. In emotional states equilibrium is lost. In a more conscious state also there would be an element of harmony or balance which could look at the situation without tipping in one direction or another.

DA: In that condition of balance, is there a special function for language? Does language have a place?

WS: Again, I would think that in a rare moment of heightened consciousness, speech would have to give way to stillness, silence. Silence is deeper than the word. "In the beginning was the word" is not entirely correct, because the void was prior to the word, and the silence precedes speech. Meister Eckhart said that prior to God is the ground of God. While the will of the Absolute is supposed to have created everything, the fact that among all creatures there are human beings with language and words is still an "improbable proposition." My friend, Peyton Houston, wrote:

The solitary person deals with a perpetual
   unintelligibility
in words without a language.

Speaking of creation, how about Peyton's vision:

How deftly she moved
when first from God's hand;
his Heart held ten thousand hummingbirds;
tall sky, sun.
He would reach to it, to all of it, to her,
speak words to her.
She taught him the language of his words;
between them was the coherent notion.

DA: Is there a secret attribute of language that makes it come alive so suddenly?

WS: Well, "alive" partakes of originality and humor too. The poet Paul Reps wrote of "cucumbers cucumbering." Such originality touches our sense of humor, wakes us up, starts fresh flows of energy. Like children, we want surprise, the unexpected. Some people have a gift for that.

DA: You've mentioned "gift" a lot, this almost organic knowledge of inner intervals and tempos and so forth. It is true that the genius is born with the gift. Goethe says that the gift of attention is the only thing that differentiates the genius from the human being. Is there a way in which I could practice developing the sensibility and the sensitivity to speak with the kind of freshness which now is missing?

WS: It's as if there is a center that can vivify all parts of the circumference—a center that illuminates. When we speak and listen from this center, a relationship is set up where words have more meaning. A hitherto unused energy is added. Most people speak, as the expression goes, from the top of their heads, so the words issue mechanically—dead words. A stop, a moment of pause, brings unsuspected energies. There is a change, the quality of energy that's transferred is quite different. It's fresh. But that is not so easy. It's easier to speak from our knowledge, from accumulated experience, from imitation of others.

DA: Is there a courageous stance towards the unknown that is required?

WS: There's a risk. At the beginning, when one speaks from this center, one feels awkward, as if one has lost the support of the known. To remain related to the unknown, at the same time keeping in touch with the knowledge that one has accumulated through experience and education, is not so easy. Still, if one lived more from one's center, one would speak with more sincerity, would find unexpected resources within oneself. One might even open in oneself conduits of expression and of material which are pretty well closed in us. One would tap material which is now dormant. Combinations of impressions would come together to produce more original, more effective language.

DA: So we need to move out of the way and allow the speaking to come on its own?

WS: Speaking from the center would be like that. It involves a kind of all-embracing attention. One would, while speaking, be quite aware, at each moment, of a center which, while doing nothing, affects all things. It may be likened to the reality self—changeless, it moves all things. Can one be aware of this element of consciousness while speaking, listening? Functioning from such a center would result in more genuine, more effective expression of thoughts and feelings. Living from this center will not make a poet of one, but it would maximize possibilities as a human being. Remembering that there is a conscious element in oneself is better than not remembering.

There is a stillness to which I can relate.
My mind and my body need this stillness to come together.
I try to open, let my body decontract to free itself.
I am patient.
I can let go more.
I let my attention relate to different parts.
The right side, the left side.
I see the relation of attention to breathing, equilibrium.

V

THE TEN OXHERDING PICTURES

The Ten Oxherding Pictures, which entered traditional literature centuries ago, are familiar to many adherents of training in self-awareness. Since the first versions appeared, there have been others, some sticking closely to the early renderings by Kaku-an, Fumyo, Itoku and the unknown author of The Ten White Ox Pictures; still other versions bear their own meaning. In the present post-modern age, with ideas swiftly exchangeable, interest in the Ox approach continues to grow. Men and women, questioning and searching, are not unreceptive to guideposts leading back to the source, to the experience of another relationship with oneself and the world.

The Way of Zen

The meaning and spirit of the oriental allegory, originating in the twelfth century as a training guide for Chinese Buddhist monks, has managed to survive many versions and interpretations. It is still used today as a teaching manual in zen monasteries in Japan. But the experience it portrays is not exclusively Zen.

People look for the Way in all directions—their search may bring them to the ends of the earth. But the way, it is indicated, is not far. It is as near as oneself, as close as one's breath. The way itself lies in wait for the seeker. The spell of open sesame, of finding the treasure that is inside and right in front of one, repeats itself in all traditions. The seeker's core of difficulty is that he cannot know what he is looking for until he finds it.

The earliest versions of the allegory ended with the empty circle. But Kaku-an Shi-en, a Zen master of the Sung dynasty, realized that this was not the end of the story. It had to be shown that from the beginning the ox had never been missing. And further, the ultimate stage of the search was neither the void nor nirvana, but the return of the enlightened seeker to the world of men and women, of all living creatures.

There is a stage of development where detachment and compassion, like eternity and time, are not incompatible. Humanity is not distinct from divinity. The quest is not merely to discover the treasure for oneself, but to share it with others, to go barefooted and open-handed to the marketplace.

The last picture may well be presented with the first, for neither age nor cognitive development need enter into moments of sageness. The novice, everyman, may experience the vision lived as a continuum by the master.

Still, the appearance of a developed awareness depends on right knowledge, on persistent training of the physical, the emotional, and the intellectual parts. Sagely being is not founded on youthful laziness. The search begins with the infant's first breath, bearing the query: "Whoam I...where...whence?" Drop by drop, step by step, effort by effort, one develops capacities to remain open to the myriad miracles of the moment.

Awareness of awareness dropped off, the old man is each one of us in right relationship to a sacred universe. Subject to the laws of earth, of time, of old age, illness, and death, undifferentiated, unborn energy radiates through his organism. For him, no time exists, no space. He is both father and child of the novice figure in the first picture.

The oxherding theme is simple. But at the same time it is profound and subtle, pointing to the ultimate meaning of man's existence on earth. What could be more simple than a man looking for his ox? But when we realize what the ox is, what could be more profound?

To find out who one is, and to know that the ox is never missing, is not easy. Difficult to describe the experience through pictures. Still, we can look at them with an open heart. Then...maybe.

Child and master
Worlds apart
Essentially the same.

We are all
The one master
Potentially, actually.

Aware of Self
Aware of self
Forgotten is self.

Not bound by past
Nor future beckoned
Now.

THE TEN OXHERDING PICTURES

SEARCHING FOR THE OX: the boy has only vague presentiments of its existence. The beast has never gone astray and what is the use of searching? The reason why the oxherd is not on intimate terms with him is because the oxherd has violated his own innermost nature. The beast is lost, for the oxherd has been led out of the way through his deluding senses. His home is receding farther from him, confused by byways and crossways.

Alone in the wilderness, lost in the jungle,
  the boy is searching, searching!
The swelling waters, the far away mountains,
  and the unending path;
Exhausted and in despair, he knows not
  where to go,
He only hears the evening cicadas singing
  in the maple woods.

FINDING THE TRACKS: in writings and in teachings he begins to get clues. By the aid of the scriptures and by inquiring into the doctrines, he has come to understand something; he has found the traces. He now knows that vessels, however varied in form, are all of gold, and that the objective world is a reflection of the Self. Yet, he is unable to distinguish what is good from what is not, his mind is still confused as to truth and falsehood.

*By the stream and under the trees,
    scattered are the traces of the lost;
The sweet-scented grasses are growing
    thick—did he find the way?
However remote over the hills and far
    away the beast may wander,
His nose reaches the heavens.*

SEEING THE OX: he begins to have a glimpse of his own reality. The boy finds the way by the sound he hears; all his senses are in harmonious order; he sees thereby into the origin of things. In all his activities, it is manifest. It is like the salt in water and like glue in color. It is there although not distinguishable as an individual entity. When the eye is properly directed, he will find that it is no other than himself.

*On a yonder branch perches a nightingale
  cheerfully singing;
The sun is warm, and a soothing breeze
  blows; on the bank the willows are green.
The ox is there all by himself, nowhere
  is there a place to hide.
The splendid head decorated with stately
  horns—what painter can portray him?*

CATCHING THE OX: long lost in the wilderness, the boy has at last found the ox and his hands are on him. But, owing to the overwhelming pressure of the outside world, the ox is hard to keep under control. Constantly he longs for the old sweet-scented field. His wild nature is still unruly, and altogether refuses to be broken.

*With the energy of his whole being, the
  boy has at last taken hold of the ox:
But how wild the ox's will, how ungovernable
  his power!
At times he paces upon the plateau,
When lo! he is lost again in a misty
  impenetrable mountain pass.*

HERDING THE OX: when a thought moves, another follows, and then another—an endless train of thoughts is thus awakened. Through enlightenment all this turns into truth; but falsehood asserts itself when confusion prevails. Things oppress us not because of an objective world, but because of a self-deceiving mind.

The boy is not to separate himself from
  his whip and tether,
Lest the animal should wander away into
  a world of defilements;
When he is properly tended to, the ox will
  grow pure and docile;
Without a chain, nothing binding, he will
  by himself follow the oxherd.

COMING HOME: on the ox's back he tunefully and leisurely plays his flute. The struggle is over; with gain and loss, the man is no more concerned. He hums a rustic woodman's tune; he sings a simple village boy's song. Straddling the ox's back, his eyes are fixed on things not of the earth. Even if he is called, he will not turn his head; however enticed he will not look back.

*Riding on the animal, he leisurely wends
    his way home:
Enveloped in the evening mist, how tunefully
    the flute dies away!
Singing a ditty, beating time, his heart is
    filled with indescribable joy!
That he is now one of those who know—
    need it be told?*

LO, THE OX IS NO MORE: the boy's whip and rope idly lying about—not needed. The ox is symbolic. When you know that what you need is not the snare or net but the hare or fish, it is like gold separated from the dross, or the moon rising out of the clouds. The one ray of light, serene and penetrating, has always shone—even before days of creation.

VII

*Riding on the animal, he is at last back
 in his home,
Where lo! the ox is no more. The man
 alone sits serenely.
Under a straw-thatched roof are his whip
 and rope idly lying.
Though the red sun is high in the sky,
 he is still quietly dreaming.*

GONE, GONE, ALTOGETHER GONE: the boy and the ox are both gone. The boy's confusion has been set aside and serenity alone prevails; even the idea of holiness does not obtain. He does not linger about where the Buddha is, and where there is no Buddha he speedily passes by. When no dualism, no forms exist, even a thousand eyes fail to detect a loophole.

*All is empty—the whip, the rope, the
  man, and the ox:
Who can ever survey the vastness of
  heaven?
Over the furnace burning ablaze, not a
  flake of snow can fall:
When this state of things obtains, manifest
  is the spirit of the ancient master.*

BACK TO THE SOURCE: he is neither for nor against the transformations that are going on. From the very beginning, pure and immaculate, the man has never been affected by defilement. He watches the growth of things, while himself abiding in the immovable serenity of nonassertion. He does not identify himself with the transformations that are going on about him.

*To return to the origin, to be back at the
    source—already a false step this!
Far better it is to stay home, blind and
    deaf, and without much ado;
Sitting in the hut, he takes no cognizance
    of things outside.
Behold the streams flowing—whither nobody
    knows; and the flowers vividly
    red—for whom are they?*

THE OLD MAN IN THE MARKET: no glimpses of his inner life are to be caught—barefooted he goes to the marketplace. His cottage gate is closed, and even the wisest know him not, for he goes on his own way without following the steps of the ancient sages. Carrying a bowl he goes out into the marketplace, leaning against a staff he comes home.

*Barechested and barefooted, he comes
  out into the marketplace;
Daubed with mud and ashes, how broadly
  he smiles!
There is no need for the miraculous power
  of the gods,
For he touches, and lo! the dead trees are
  in full bloom.*

UNATTENDED, body/mind/feelings dominate and blur an ever-present inner reality, inevitably distorting man's correct view of his situations and his destiny.

Nonetheless, Self—I—Master is always present. We are 'that,' and as many teachings insist, 'that' will remain when man's structure disintegrates.

At moments of silent contemplation, when attention is strongly held and more open to an inner world, the taste of unity may appear. The single biggest barrier, for the beginner as well as advanced seeker, is the illusion that we are only this body reading these words.

Riding on Realty itself, the boy, like all of us, is always within the circle. From beginning to end, he has never left it.

*The Circle
Is—always.
The Boy seeks
What has
Never been*

Lost.

*How to find
What cannot
Be found
Until it is*

Found.

*Waking up
For a moment
May reveal
One has slept
For the hour.*

*Seeing that
One is not*

*First step
Toward seeing*

One is.

Sitting still — I am
Moving — I am
Looking up — I am
Turning head — I am
Breathing in — I am
Breathing out — I am
Seeing tension — I am
Letting go — I am
Touching you — I am
Silent — I am

I AM

ONE SOUND PENETRATES THE WHOLE UNIVERSE.

Much of the material in this book first appeared in a five-volume series of limited edition, fine press monographs. Long out of circulation, Volume I, *The Middle Ground*, was published in September of 1985. It was followed by *The Structure of Man* (1987), *The Ten Oxherding Pictures* (1988), *Opening* (1993), and *Meetings with Three Tibetan Masters* (1995). Additional material was taken from previously unpublished writings by William Segal. All illustrations are by the author. This book, like the originals, is set in Bembo. Much gratitude is due to all of those who played a part in the creation of the original series of monographs, and to those who helped make this book possible.

Green River Press • Stillgate Publishers • Sunderland, Massachusetts